50 Thailand Cuisine Recipes for Home

By: Kelly Johnson

Table of Contents

- Pad Thai
- Green Curry Chicken
- Tom Yum Soup
- Massaman Curry
- Som Tum (Green Papaya Salad)
- Pad Kra Pao (Basil Chicken)
- Tom Kha Gai (Coconut Chicken Soup)
- Red Curry Beef
- Pineapple Fried Rice
- Pad See Ew (Stir-Fried Noodles)
- Mango Sticky Rice
- Larb Gai (Minced Chicken Salad)
- Panang Curry
- Chicken Satay with Peanut Sauce
- Thai Iced Tea
- Gaeng Keow Wan Gai (Green Chicken Curry)
- Khao Soi (Northern Thai Curry Noodles)
- Pad Prik Khing (Stir-Fried Red Curry Paste)
- Moo Pad Krapow (Stir-Fried Pork with Basil)
- Drunken Noodles (Pad Kee Mao)
- Yum Woon Sen (Glass Noodle Salad)
- Grilled Lemongrass Chicken
- Thai Basil Fried Rice
- Thai Red Curry Shrimp
- Nam Prik Ong (Northern Thai Chili Dip)
- Pla Rad Prik (Fried Fish with Chili Sauce)
- Panang Moo Tod (Panang Curry Pork)
- Thai Crab Fried Rice
- Green Papaya Soup with Pork Ribs
- Pad Cha Talay (Seafood Stir-Fry)
- Pad Ped Moo (Spicy Stir-Fried Pork)
- Nam Tok Moo (Grilled Pork Salad)
- Pla Tod Kamin (Turmeric Fried Fish)
- Thai Coconut Ice Cream
- Pad Ma Kuer Yao (Stir-Fried Eggplant)

- Khanom Krok (Coconut Pancakes)
- Chicken and Cashew Nut Stir-Fry
- Thai Beef Salad
- Gaeng Som (Sour Curry)
- Kanom Jeen Nam Ya (Rice Noodles with Fish Curry)
- Kai Jeow Moo Sab (Pork Omelette)
- Kao Niew Mamuang (Mango Sticky Rice)
- Gang Hung Lay (Northern Thai Pork Curry)
- Hoy Tod (Thai Mussels Pancake)
- Kaeng Liang (Vegetable Soup)
- Pad Phrik Khing Tofu (Stir-Fried Tofu)
- Gaeng Om (Northern Thai Curry Soup)
- Pla Nung Manao (Steamed Fish with Lime)
- Khao Khluk Kapi (Fried Rice with Shrimp Paste)
- Thai Custard (Sangkhaya)

Pad Thai

Ingredients:

- 8 oz (about 225g) rice noodles
- 2 tablespoons tamarind paste
- 3 tablespoons fish sauce
- 1 tablespoon soy sauce
- 1 tablespoon oyster sauce
- 1 tablespoon sugar
- 2 tablespoons vegetable oil
- 1/2 cup firm tofu, cubed
- 2 cloves garlic, minced
- 1/2 cup shrimp, peeled and deveined (optional)
- 2 eggs, lightly beaten
- 2 cups bean sprouts
- 3 green onions, chopped
- 1/4 cup crushed peanuts
- Lime wedges for serving

Instructions:

Prepare Rice Noodles:
    Cook the rice noodles according to the package instructions. Drain and set aside.

Make Pad Thai Sauce:
    In a small bowl, mix tamarind paste, fish sauce, soy sauce, oyster sauce, and sugar to create the Pad Thai sauce. Adjust the sweetness or tanginess to your liking.

Stir-Fry Tofu:
    Heat vegetable oil in a wok or large skillet over medium-high heat. Add cubed tofu and stir-fry until golden brown. Remove tofu from the wok and set aside.

Cook Garlic and Shrimp:
    In the same wok, add minced garlic and stir-fry for about 30 seconds until fragrant. If using shrimp, add them to the wok and cook until they turn pink and opaque.

Push Ingredients to the Side:
　　Push the ingredients to one side of the wok and pour the beaten eggs into the other side. Scramble the eggs until they are mostly cooked.

Combine Ingredients:
　　Mix the cooked tofu and rice noodles into the wok, combining all the ingredients.

Add Pad Thai Sauce:
　　Pour the Pad Thai sauce over the noodles and toss everything together until well-coated. Cook for an additional 2-3 minutes.

Add Bean Sprouts and Green Onions:
　　Add bean sprouts and chopped green onions to the wok. Toss for another minute until the bean sprouts are slightly cooked but still crunchy.

Serve:
　　Serve the Pad Thai hot, garnished with crushed peanuts and lime wedges on the side.

Garnish and Enjoy:
　　Garnish with additional bean sprouts, chopped green onions, crushed peanuts, and a squeeze of lime juice before serving.

Enjoy your homemade Pad Thai with the perfect balance of sweet, savory, and tangy flavors! Feel free to customize it by adding more vegetables, protein, or adjusting the level of spiciness to suit your taste.

Green Curry Chicken

Ingredients:

For the Green Curry Paste:

- 2 green Thai chilies (adjust to taste)
- 2 shallots, peeled and chopped
- 3 cloves garlic, peeled
- 1 lemongrass stalk, thinly sliced (white part only)
- 1 thumb-sized piece of galangal or ginger, peeled and chopped
- 1 teaspoon ground coriander
- 1/2 teaspoon ground cumin
- 1/2 teaspoon shrimp paste (optional)
- Zest of 1 lime
- 1/4 cup fresh cilantro leaves and stems, chopped
- 2 tablespoons fresh basil leaves
- 1 tablespoon fish sauce
- 1 tablespoon soy sauce
- 1 tablespoon vegetable oil

For the Green Curry Chicken:

- 1 pound (450g) boneless, skinless chicken thighs, cut into bite-sized pieces
- 2 tablespoons green curry paste (homemade or store-bought)
- 1 can (14 oz) coconut milk
- 1 cup chicken broth
- 1 tablespoon vegetable oil
- 1 red bell pepper, sliced
- 1 cup Thai eggplants or regular eggplants, sliced
- 1 cup bamboo shoots, sliced (optional)
- Fresh basil leaves for garnish
- Cooked jasmine rice for serving

Instructions:

For the Green Curry Paste:

Prepare Ingredients:

Gather all the ingredients for the green curry paste.

Blend:

In a blender or food processor, blend all the green curry paste ingredients until you achieve a smooth and vibrant green paste. Add a little water if needed.

For the Green Curry Chicken:

Cook Chicken:

Heat vegetable oil in a large pot or wok over medium heat. Add the green curry paste and cook for a couple of minutes until fragrant.

Add Chicken:

Add the chicken pieces and cook until they are browned on all sides.

Pour Coconut Milk:

Pour in the coconut milk and chicken broth. Bring the mixture to a gentle simmer.

Add Vegetables:

Add the sliced red bell pepper, Thai eggplants, and bamboo shoots. Simmer until the vegetables are tender and the chicken is cooked through.

Season:

Taste the curry and adjust the seasoning with more fish sauce or soy sauce if needed.

Serve:

Serve the Green Curry Chicken over cooked jasmine rice. Garnish with fresh basil leaves.

Enjoy:

Enjoy your homemade Green Curry Chicken, savoring the aromatic and flavorful Thai green curry!

Feel free to customize the recipe by adding other vegetables or adjusting the spice level according to your preference.

Tom Yum Soup

Ingredients:

For the Soup Base:

- 4 cups chicken or vegetable broth
- 1 lemongrass stalk, cut into 2-inch pieces and smashed
- 3-4 kaffir lime leaves, torn into pieces
- 2-3 Thai bird's eye chilies, smashed (adjust to taste)
- 3 slices galangal or ginger
- 2 cloves garlic, smashed
- 1 medium-sized tomato, quartered
- 200g (7 oz) shrimp, peeled and deveined
- 200g (7 oz) mushrooms, sliced
- 1 medium-sized onion, sliced
- 1 tablespoon fish sauce (adjust to taste)
- 1 tablespoon soy sauce
- 1 tablespoon lime juice (adjust to taste)
- 1 teaspoon sugar (optional)

Optional Ingredients:

- Thai chili paste (Nam Prik Pao) for extra heat (optional)
- Fresh cilantro leaves for garnish
- Spring onions, sliced, for garnish
- Thai bird's eye chilies, sliced, for garnish

Instructions:

Prepare Ingredients:
Gather and prepare all the ingredients for the soup.

Make Soup Base:
In a pot, bring the chicken or vegetable broth to a simmer. Add lemongrass, kaffir lime leaves, bird's eye chilies, galangal or ginger, garlic, and tomatoes. Let it simmer for about 5-7 minutes to infuse the flavors.

Add Vegetables:
Add sliced mushrooms and onions to the pot. Simmer until the vegetables are tender.

Add Shrimp:
Add peeled and deveined shrimp to the pot. Cook until the shrimp turn pink and opaque.

Season:
Season the soup with fish sauce, soy sauce, lime juice, and sugar (if using). Adjust the seasoning to achieve the desired balance of spicy, sour, and salty flavors.

Optional Chili Paste:
If you prefer more heat, you can add Thai chili paste (Nam Prik Pao) to the soup.

Remove Aromatics:
Remove lemongrass, kaffir lime leaves, galangal or ginger slices, and garlic from the soup.

Garnish and Serve:
Ladle the Tom Yum Soup into bowls. Garnish with fresh cilantro leaves, sliced spring onions, and additional sliced bird's eye chilies if you like.

Serve Hot:
Serve the Tom Yum Soup hot and enjoy the bold and zesty flavors.

Tom Yum Soup is a versatile dish, and you can customize it by adding your favorite protein or vegetables. Whether you prefer it with shrimp, chicken, or tofu, this Thai soup is sure to tantalize your taste buds with its delicious combination of spicy and sour elements.

Massaman Curry

Ingredients:

For the Massaman Curry Paste:

- 1 large onion, chopped
- 4 cloves garlic, minced
- 2 tablespoons galangal or ginger, chopped
- 2 tablespoons lemongrass, sliced
- 1 teaspoon shrimp paste (optional)
- 1 teaspoon ground coriander
- 1 teaspoon ground cumin
- 1/2 teaspoon ground cinnamon
- 1/2 teaspoon ground cardamom
- 1/2 teaspoon ground cloves
- 1/2 teaspoon ground nutmeg
- 4-6 dried red chili peppers, soaked in warm water
- 2 tablespoons vegetable oil

For the Massaman Curry:

- 1 pound (450g) beef or chicken, cut into bite-sized pieces
- 2 cans (800ml) coconut milk
- 1 cup chicken or beef broth
- 2 potatoes, peeled and cut into chunks
- 1 large carrot, sliced
- 1 onion, sliced
- 1/2 cup roasted peanuts
- 3 tablespoons Massaman Curry Paste (from above)
- 2 tablespoons fish sauce
- 1 tablespoon tamarind paste
- 1-2 tablespoons palm sugar or brown sugar (adjust to taste)
- 1 cinnamon stick
- 3-4 cardamom pods
- 3-4 bay leaves
- Salt, to taste
- Fresh cilantro for garnish

Instructions:

For the Massaman Curry Paste:

Prepare Ingredients:
> Gather and prepare all the ingredients for the Massaman Curry paste.

Blend:
> In a food processor or blender, blend all the Massaman Curry paste ingredients until you achieve a smooth and aromatic paste.

For the Massaman Curry:

Cook Beef or Chicken:
> In a large pot or wok, heat a couple of tablespoons of coconut milk over medium heat. Add the Massaman Curry paste and cook for a few minutes until fragrant.

Add Meat:
> Add the beef or chicken pieces and cook until they are browned on all sides.

Add Coconut Milk:
> Pour in the remaining coconut milk and chicken or beef broth. Bring the mixture to a simmer.

Add Vegetables:
> Add potatoes, carrots, and sliced onions to the pot. Stir well.

Season:
> Season the curry with fish sauce, tamarind paste, palm sugar or brown sugar, cinnamon stick, cardamom pods, bay leaves, and salt. Adjust the seasoning to your taste.

Simmer:
> Let the Massaman Curry simmer over low heat for about 30-40 minutes or until the meat is tender, and the flavors have melded together.

Add Peanuts:
> Add roasted peanuts to the curry and cook for an additional 10 minutes.

Remove Aromatics:
> Remove cinnamon stick, cardamom pods, and bay leaves from the curry.

Garnish and Serve:
> Garnish the Massaman Curry with fresh cilantro and serve it hot over jasmine rice.

Enjoy the rich and comforting flavors of homemade Massaman Curry, a Thai curry that is both hearty and aromatic. Adjust the level of spiciness and sweetness according to your preferences.

Som Tum (Green Papaya Salad)

Ingredients:

- 2 cups shredded green papaya
- 1 cup cherry tomatoes, halved
- 1 cup long beans, cut into 2-inch pieces
- 2-3 Thai bird's eye chilies, chopped (adjust to taste)
- 2 cloves garlic, minced
- 1/4 cup roasted peanuts, coarsely crushed
- 2 tablespoons dried shrimp (optional)
- 2 tablespoons fish sauce
- 1.5 tablespoons palm sugar or brown sugar
- 2 tablespoons lime juice
- 2 tablespoons tamarind paste
- 2 tablespoons dried shrimp (optional)
- 1-2 tablespoons fish sauce (adjust to taste)
- Fresh cilantro for garnish
- Lime wedges for serving

Instructions:

Prepare Green Papaya:

Peel and shred the green papaya using a grater or a julienne peeler. Place the shredded papaya in a large mixing bowl.

Prepare Vegetables:

Add halved cherry tomatoes and cut long beans to the bowl with shredded papaya.

Make Dressing:

In a separate bowl, combine chopped Thai chilies, minced garlic, roasted peanuts, dried shrimp (if using), fish sauce, palm sugar, lime juice, and tamarind paste. Mix well until the sugar is dissolved.

Toss Salad:

Pour the dressing over the shredded papaya and vegetables. Toss everything together until well coated.

Adjust Seasoning:

Taste the salad and adjust the seasoning as needed. You can add more fish sauce for saltiness, lime juice for acidity, or sugar for sweetness.

Serve:

Transfer the Som Tum to a serving plate and garnish with fresh cilantro.

Garnish and Serve:

Garnish with additional crushed peanuts and serve the Som Tum with lime wedges on the side.

Enjoy the refreshing and zesty flavors of Som Tum as a side dish or a light meal. The combination of crunchy green papaya, juicy tomatoes, and the flavorful dressing makes this Thai salad a delightful and satisfying option. Adjust the spice level and other ingredients according to your preferences.

Pad Kra Pao (Basil Chicken)

Ingredients:

- 1 pound (450g) ground chicken or thinly sliced chicken breast
- 2 tablespoons vegetable oil
- 4 cloves garlic, minced
- 3-4 Thai bird's eye chilies, chopped (adjust to taste)
- 1 cup fresh basil leaves (Thai basil is preferable)
- 1 tablespoon oyster sauce
- 1 tablespoon soy sauce
- 1 teaspoon fish sauce
- 1 teaspoon sugar
- Lime wedges for serving
- Fried egg (optional) for serving
- Jasmine rice for serving

Instructions:

Prepare Ingredients:

Gather and prepare all the ingredients for the Pad Kra Pao.

Stir-Fry Chicken:

Heat vegetable oil in a wok or a large skillet over medium-high heat. Add minced garlic and chopped Thai bird's eye chilies. Stir-fry for about 30 seconds until fragrant.

Add Chicken:

Add ground chicken or thinly sliced chicken breast to the wok. Stir-fry until the chicken is cooked through and browned.

Season with Sauces:

Add oyster sauce, soy sauce, fish sauce, and sugar to the chicken. Stir well to combine.

Add Basil Leaves:

Add fresh basil leaves to the wok. Stir-fry for an additional 1-2 minutes until the basil is wilted.

Taste and Adjust:

Taste the Pad Kra Pao and adjust the seasoning if needed. You can add more soy sauce, fish sauce, or sugar to balance the flavors.

Serve:

Serve the Pad Kra Pao over jasmine rice. Optionally, top it with a fried egg.

Garnish and Serve:

Garnish with additional basil leaves and serve the Pad Kra Pao hot. Provide lime wedges on the side for squeezing over the dish.

Enjoy the bold and aromatic flavors of Pad Kra Pao, a quick and delicious Thai stir-fry. The combination of fragrant basil, spicy chilies, and savory sauce makes this dish a favorite for many Thai food enthusiasts. Adjust the level of spiciness according to your taste preferences.

Tom Kha Gai (Coconut Chicken Soup)

Ingredients:

- 1 pound (450g) boneless, skinless chicken thighs, thinly sliced
- 4 cups chicken broth
- 1 can (14 oz) coconut milk
- 1 lemongrass stalk, cut into 2-inch pieces and smashed
- 3-4 kaffir lime leaves, torn into pieces
- 2-3 Thai bird's eye chilies, smashed (adjust to taste)
- 1 thumb-sized piece of galangal or ginger, sliced
- 3 tablespoons fish sauce
- 2 tablespoons lime juice
- 1 tablespoon palm sugar or brown sugar
- 1 cup mushrooms, sliced
- 1 medium-sized tomato, sliced
- Fresh cilantro leaves for garnish
- Fresh Thai basil leaves for garnish (optional)
- Lime wedges for serving

Instructions:

Prepare Ingredients:
    Gather and prepare all the ingredients for Tom Kha Gai.

Make Broth:
    In a pot, bring the chicken broth to a simmer. Add lemongrass, kaffir lime leaves, Thai bird's eye chilies, and galangal or ginger. Let it simmer for about 10-15 minutes to infuse the flavors.

Add Chicken:
    Add the thinly sliced chicken thighs to the pot. Cook until the chicken is cooked through.

Add Coconut Milk:
    Pour in the coconut milk and bring the soup back to a gentle simmer.

Season:

Season the soup with fish sauce, lime juice, and palm sugar or brown sugar. Adjust the seasoning to achieve the desired balance of sweet, sour, and salty flavors.

Add Vegetables:
Add sliced mushrooms and tomato to the soup. Simmer until the vegetables are tender.

Remove Aromatics:
Remove lemongrass, kaffir lime leaves, Thai bird's eye chilies, and galangal or ginger slices from the soup.

Garnish:
Garnish the Tom Kha Gai with fresh cilantro leaves and, optionally, Thai basil leaves.

Serve:
Serve the Tom Kha Gai hot, and provide lime wedges on the side for squeezing over the soup.

Enjoy the comforting and creamy flavors of homemade Tom Kha Gai. This Thai coconut chicken soup is perfect for warming up on a chilly day or as a delightful appetizer before your main meal. Adjust the level of spiciness and sweetness according to your preferences.

Red Curry Beef

Ingredients:

For the Red Curry Paste:

- 4-6 dried red chili peppers, soaked in warm water
- 1 shallot, chopped
- 4 cloves garlic, minced
- 1 thumb-sized piece of galangal or ginger, sliced
- 1 lemongrass stalk, thinly sliced (white part only)
- 1 teaspoon ground coriander
- 1/2 teaspoon ground cumin
- 1/2 teaspoon shrimp paste (optional)
- 1/2 teaspoon ground paprika (for color)
- 1/4 teaspoon ground white pepper
- 2 tablespoons vegetable oil

For the Red Curry Beef:

- 1 pound (450g) beef sirloin or flank steak, thinly sliced
- 2 tablespoons vegetable oil
- 1 can (14 oz) coconut milk
- 2-3 tablespoons red curry paste (from above)
- 1 tablespoon fish sauce
- 1 tablespoon soy sauce
- 1 tablespoon palm sugar or brown sugar
- 1 bell pepper, sliced
- 1 zucchini, sliced
- Fresh basil leaves for garnish
- Jasmine rice for serving

Instructions:

For the Red Curry Paste:

Prepare Ingredients:
    Gather and prepare all the ingredients for the Red Curry Paste.

Blend:

In a food processor or blender, blend all the Red Curry Paste ingredients until you achieve a smooth and vibrant red paste.

For the Red Curry Beef:

Prepare Beef:
Thinly slice the beef and set aside.

Cook Red Curry Paste:
Heat vegetable oil in a wok or large skillet over medium-high heat. Add 2-3 tablespoons of the Red Curry Paste and stir-fry for a couple of minutes until fragrant.

Add Beef:
Add the sliced beef to the wok and cook until browned on all sides.

Add Coconut Milk:
Pour in the coconut milk, fish sauce, soy sauce, and palm sugar. Stir well to combine.

Add Vegetables:
Add sliced bell pepper and zucchini to the wok. Simmer until the vegetables are tender, and the beef is cooked through.

Adjust Seasoning:
Taste the Red Curry Beef and adjust the seasoning if needed. You can add more fish sauce, soy sauce, or sugar to balance the flavors.

Garnish:
Garnish the Red Curry Beef with fresh basil leaves.

Serve:
Serve the Red Curry Beef hot over jasmine rice.

Enjoy the bold and spicy flavors of homemade Red Curry Beef, a classic Thai dish that is both comforting and satisfying. Adjust the level of spiciness and sweetness according to your preferences.

Pineapple Fried Rice

Ingredients:

- 3 cups cooked jasmine rice (preferably cold and day-old)
- 1 cup pineapple chunks, fresh or canned
- 1/2 cup cooked and diced chicken (optional)
- 1/2 cup cooked and peeled shrimp (optional)
- 1/2 cup diced ham
- 1/2 cup cashews or peanuts, roasted
- 1/2 cup frozen peas, thawed
- 1/2 cup carrot, diced
- 1/2 cup red bell pepper, diced
- 2 cloves garlic, minced
- 2 eggs, beaten
- 3 tablespoons soy sauce
- 1 tablespoon fish sauce
- 1 tablespoon oyster sauce
- 1 tablespoon curry powder
- 2 green onions, chopped
- Fresh cilantro for garnish
- Lime wedges for serving

Instructions:

Prepare Ingredients:
    Cook the jasmine rice in advance and let it cool. Gather and prepare all the ingredients for Pineapple Fried Rice.

Stir-Fry Aromatics:
    Heat a wok or a large skillet over medium-high heat. Add a bit of oil and sauté minced garlic until fragrant.

Add Chicken and Shrimp (Optional):
    If using chicken or shrimp, add them to the wok and stir-fry until cooked through.

Cook Vegetables:
    Add diced ham, pineapple chunks, peas, carrot, and red bell pepper to the wok.
    Stir-fry for a few minutes until the vegetables are tender.

Push Ingredients to the Side:
Push the ingredients to one side of the wok, and pour the beaten eggs into the other side. Scramble the eggs until they are mostly cooked.

Combine Ingredients:
Mix the cooked jasmine rice into the wok with the scrambled eggs and other ingredients. Stir well to combine.

Add Sauce and Seasoning:
Pour soy sauce, fish sauce, oyster sauce, and curry powder over the rice mixture. Stir-fry until everything is evenly coated and heated through.

Add Nuts and Green Onions:
Add roasted cashews or peanuts and chopped green onions to the wok. Stir to incorporate.

Taste and Adjust:
Taste the Pineapple Fried Rice and adjust the seasoning if needed. You can add more soy sauce or fish sauce according to your preference.

Garnish and Serve:
Garnish the Pineapple Fried Rice with fresh cilantro and serve it hot. Provide lime wedges on the side for squeezing over the rice.

Enjoy the delightful combination of sweet pineapple, savory meat, and aromatic spices in this Pineapple Fried Rice. It's a colorful and satisfying dish that's perfect for a quick and flavorful meal.

Pad See Ew (Stir-Fried Noodles)

Ingredients:

- 8 oz (about 225g) wide rice noodles
- 2 tablespoons vegetable oil
- 1 cup broccoli florets
- 1 cup Chinese broccoli (gai lan) or regular broccoli, sliced
- 1/2 cup carrots, thinly sliced
- 2 cloves garlic, minced
- 1 cup protein of choice (chicken, beef, shrimp, tofu), thinly sliced or diced
- 2 eggs, beaten
- 3 tablespoons soy sauce
- 2 tablespoons oyster sauce
- 1 tablespoon dark soy sauce (for color)
- 1 tablespoon fish sauce
- 1 tablespoon sugar
- White pepper, to taste
- Green onions, chopped, for garnish

Instructions:

Prepare Rice Noodles:
    Cook the wide rice noodles according to package instructions. Drain and set aside.

Stir-Fry Vegetables:
    Heat vegetable oil in a wok or large skillet over medium-high heat. Add minced garlic and stir-fry until fragrant. Add broccoli, Chinese broccoli, and carrots. Stir-fry until the vegetables are tender-crisp. Remove them from the wok and set aside.

Cook Protein:
    In the same wok, add a bit more oil if needed. Cook the sliced or diced protein (chicken, beef, shrimp, tofu) until it's fully cooked.

Push Ingredients to the Side:
    Push the protein to one side of the wok and pour the beaten eggs into the other side. Scramble the eggs until they are mostly cooked.

Combine Ingredients:
> Mix the cooked rice noodles and the stir-fried vegetables back into the wok with the cooked protein and eggs.

Make Sauce:
> In a small bowl, whisk together soy sauce, oyster sauce, dark soy sauce, fish sauce, sugar, and white pepper.

Pour Sauce Over Noodles:
> Pour the sauce over the noodle mixture in the wok. Toss everything together until the noodles are evenly coated in the sauce and heated through.

Taste and Adjust:
> Taste the Pad See Ew and adjust the seasoning if needed. You can add more soy sauce, fish sauce, or sugar according to your taste.

Garnish and Serve:
> Garnish the Pad See Ew with chopped green onions and serve it hot.

Enjoy your homemade Pad See Ew, a comforting and savory Thai stir-fried noodle dish that's quick and easy to make at home. Adjust the ingredients and protein choices to suit your preferences.

Mango Sticky Rice

Ingredients:

For Sticky Rice:

- 1 cup glutinous rice
- 1 cup coconut milk
- 1/2 cup sugar
- 1/2 teaspoon salt

For Topping:

- 2 ripe mangoes, peeled, pitted, and sliced
- Sesame seeds for garnish (optional)
- Mung beans for garnish (optional)

For Coconut Sauce:

- 1/2 cup coconut milk
- 2 tablespoons sugar
- 1/4 teaspoon salt

Instructions:

For Sticky Rice:

Soak Rice:
Rinse glutinous rice under cold water until the water runs clear. Soak the rice in water for at least 4 hours or overnight.

Steam Rice:
Drain the soaked rice and place it in a steamer lined with cheesecloth or a thin kitchen towel. Steam the rice for about 25-30 minutes or until it becomes tender and translucent.

Prepare Coconut Mixture:
While the rice is steaming, mix coconut milk, sugar, and salt in a saucepan. Heat over medium heat until the sugar dissolves. Remove from heat and set aside.

Combine Coconut Mixture:

Once the rice is cooked, transfer it to a large bowl. Pour half of the coconut milk mixture over the rice and gently fold it in until the rice is coated. Let it sit for a few minutes to allow the rice to absorb the coconut milk.

For Coconut Sauce:

Prepare Coconut Sauce:
> In a separate saucepan, combine coconut milk, sugar, and salt for the coconut sauce. Heat over medium heat until the sugar dissolves. Remove from heat.

Assembling Mango Sticky Rice:

Serve:
> Place a portion of the coconut-infused sticky rice on a serving plate.

Add Mango Slices:
> Arrange slices of ripe mango on top of the sticky rice.

Drizzle Coconut Sauce:
> Drizzle the prepared coconut sauce over the mango and rice.

Garnish:
> Optionally, garnish with sesame seeds and mung beans for added texture and presentation.

Serve Warm:
> Serve the Mango Sticky Rice warm, allowing the sweet and coconut flavors to meld together.

Enjoy the luscious and tropical delight of homemade Mango Sticky Rice. It's a delightful way to end a Thai meal or to satisfy your sweet cravings.

Larb Gai (Minced Chicken Salad)

Ingredients:

For Larb Gai:

- 1 pound (450g) ground chicken
- 2 tablespoons vegetable oil
- 1/4 cup chicken broth
- 2 shallots, finely chopped
- 3 tablespoons fish sauce
- 2 tablespoons lime juice
- 1 teaspoon sugar
- 1-2 tablespoons ground roasted rice (optional, for texture)
- 1-2 teaspoons dried chili flakes (adjust to taste)
- Fresh cilantro leaves, chopped, for garnish
- Fresh mint leaves, chopped, for garnish
- Green onions, chopped, for garnish
- Lettuce leaves, for serving

For Ground Roasted Rice (Optional):

- 2 tablespoons sticky (glutinous) rice

Instructions:

For Ground Roasted Rice (Optional):

Dry Roast Sticky Rice:
    In a dry pan over medium heat, toast the sticky rice until it becomes golden brown. Stir constantly to prevent burning.

Grind Rice:
    Once the rice is toasted, let it cool and grind it into a coarse powder using a mortar and pestle or a spice grinder.

For Larb Gai:

Cook Ground Chicken:

In a large skillet, heat vegetable oil over medium-high heat. Add ground chicken and cook until browned and fully cooked.

Add Shallots:
Add finely chopped shallots to the skillet and cook for a couple of minutes until softened.

Season with Fish Sauce:
Pour fish sauce over the chicken and stir well to combine.

Add Chicken Broth:
Pour chicken broth into the skillet and continue cooking for a few minutes until the liquid is mostly absorbed.

Add Lime Juice and Sugar:
Add lime juice and sugar to the mixture. Stir well.

Add Chili Flakes:
Adjust the spice level by adding dried chili flakes. Stir to incorporate.

Optional Ground Roasted Rice:
If using ground roasted rice, add it to the skillet and mix well for added texture.

Taste and Adjust:
Taste the Larb Gai and adjust the seasoning according to your preference. You can add more fish sauce, lime juice, or sugar.

Garnish:
Remove the skillet from heat. Stir in chopped cilantro, mint leaves, and green onions. Mix until well combined.

Serve:
Spoon the Larb Gai mixture onto a serving plate. Serve with lettuce leaves for wrapping.

Enjoy Larb Gai as a refreshing and flavorful Thai minced chicken salad. The combination of herbs, spices, and lime juice creates a vibrant and satisfying dish. Adjust the spice and seasoning levels to suit your taste.

Panang Curry

Ingredients:

For Panang Curry Paste:

- 4-6 dried red chili peppers, soaked in warm water
- 1 shallot, chopped
- 4 cloves garlic, minced
- 1 thumb-sized piece of galangal or ginger, sliced
- 1 lemongrass stalk, thinly sliced (white part only)
- 1 teaspoon ground coriander
- 1/2 teaspoon ground cumin
- 1/2 teaspoon shrimp paste (optional)
- 1/2 teaspoon ground paprika (for color)
- 1/4 teaspoon ground white pepper
- 2 tablespoons vegetable oil

For Panang Curry:

- 1 pound (450g) chicken or beef, thinly sliced
- 1 can (14 oz) coconut milk
- 3-4 tablespoons Panang Curry Paste (from above)
- 2 tablespoons fish sauce
- 1 tablespoon soy sauce
- 1 tablespoon palm sugar or brown sugar
- 1 kaffir lime leaf, torn into pieces (optional)
- Thai basil leaves for garnish (optional)
- Red chili slices for garnish (optional)
- Jasmine rice for serving

Instructions:

For Panang Curry Paste:

Prepare Ingredients:
 Gather and prepare all the ingredients for the Panang Curry Paste.

Blend:

In a food processor or blender, blend all the Panang Curry Paste ingredients until you achieve a smooth and vibrant paste.

For Panang Curry:

Cook Protein:
In a wok or large skillet, heat a bit of vegetable oil over medium-high heat. Add the sliced chicken or beef and cook until browned.

Add Panang Curry Paste:
Add 3-4 tablespoons of the Panang Curry Paste to the wok with the cooked protein. Stir-fry for a couple of minutes until fragrant.

Add Coconut Milk:
Pour in the coconut milk and bring the mixture to a gentle simmer.

Season:
Season the curry with fish sauce, soy sauce, and palm sugar. Stir well to combine.

Add Kaffir Lime Leaf:
If using kaffir lime leaf, add it to the curry for an additional layer of flavor.

Simmer:
Let the Panang Curry simmer over low heat for about 15-20 minutes, allowing the flavors to meld together.

Garnish:
Garnish the curry with Thai basil leaves and red chili slices if desired.

Serve:
Serve the Panang Curry hot over jasmine rice.

Enjoy the rich and aromatic flavors of homemade Panang Curry, a comforting Thai dish that combines creamy coconut milk with a perfect balance of savory and sweet notes. Adjust the level of spiciness and sweetness according to your preferences.

Chicken Satay with Peanut Sauce

Ingredients:

For Chicken Satay:

- 1 pound (450g) boneless, skinless chicken thighs or chicken breast, cut into thin strips

Marinade:

- 2 tablespoons soy sauce
- 2 tablespoons fish sauce
- 1 tablespoon curry powder
- 1 tablespoon turmeric powder
- 2 tablespoons brown sugar
- 1 tablespoon vegetable oil

For Peanut Sauce:

- 1 cup unsweetened coconut milk
- 1/2 cup creamy peanut butter
- 1-2 tablespoons red curry paste (adjust to taste)
- 2 tablespoons soy sauce
- 2 tablespoons brown sugar
- 1 tablespoon rice vinegar or white vinegar
- 1 teaspoon fish sauce
- Crushed peanuts for garnish (optional)
- Fresh cilantro for garnish (optional)

For Skewers:

- Bamboo skewers, soaked in water for at least 30 minutes

Instructions:

For Chicken Satay:

Prepare Marinade:
In a bowl, whisk together soy sauce, fish sauce, curry powder, turmeric powder, brown sugar, and vegetable oil to make the marinade.

Marinate Chicken:
> Place the chicken strips in the marinade, ensuring they are well-coated. Allow the chicken to marinate for at least 30 minutes, or preferably, refrigerate for a few hours or overnight.

For Peanut Sauce:

Prepare Peanut Sauce:
> In a saucepan, combine coconut milk, peanut butter, red curry paste, soy sauce, brown sugar, rice vinegar, and fish sauce. Heat over medium heat, stirring continuously until the peanut butter is melted, and the sauce is smooth.

Simmer:
> Bring the peanut sauce to a simmer, then reduce the heat to low. Simmer for 5-7 minutes, stirring occasionally, until the sauce thickens.

Adjust Consistency:
> If the sauce is too thick, you can thin it with a bit of water to reach your desired consistency. Remove from heat.

For Chicken Satay Skewers:

Skewer Chicken:
> Preheat the grill or a grill pan. Thread the marinated chicken strips onto soaked bamboo skewers.

Grill Chicken:
> Grill the chicken skewers over medium-high heat for about 3-4 minutes per side or until fully cooked and nicely charred.

Serve:
> Serve the Chicken Satay skewers with warm Peanut Sauce on the side.

Garnish:
> Optionally, garnish the Chicken Satay with crushed peanuts and fresh cilantro.

Enjoy the delightful combination of tender and flavorful Chicken Satay paired with a rich and savory Peanut Sauce. It makes for a perfect appetizer or main course for any occasion. Adjust the level of spiciness in both the marinade and peanut sauce according to your preference.

Thai Iced Tea

Ingredients:

- 4-5 tablespoons Thai tea leaves (or black tea leaves)
- 4 cups water
- 1/2 cup sweetened condensed milk
- 2-3 tablespoons evaporated milk or half-and-half
- Ice cubes

Instructions:

Brew Thai Tea:
- In a heatproof container, bring 4 cups of water to a boil.
- Add Thai tea leaves (or black tea leaves) to the boiling water.
- Let the tea steep for about 5-10 minutes, depending on your desired strength. Strain the tea to remove the leaves.

Sweeten the Tea:
- While the tea is still hot, stir in sweetened condensed milk. Adjust the sweetness to your liking. The more condensed milk you add, the sweeter the tea will be.

Cool the Tea:
- Allow the sweetened tea to cool to room temperature. You can place it in the refrigerator to speed up the process.

Serve over Ice:
- Fill glasses with ice cubes.
- Pour the cooled and sweetened tea over the ice.

Add Evaporated Milk:
- Top each glass with a drizzle of evaporated milk or half-and-half. Stir gently to combine.

Optional: Garnish
- Garnish with a sprig of mint or a slice of orange if desired.

Serve Cold:
- Thai Iced Tea is traditionally served cold. Enjoy it on a hot day or as a refreshing treat.

Adjust the sweetness and creaminess of the Thai Iced Tea to suit your taste. It's a delightful and indulgent beverage that pairs well with spicy Thai dishes.

Gaeng Keow Wan Gai (Green Chicken Curry)

Ingredients:

For Green Curry Paste:

- 2 green bird's eye chilies (adjust to taste)
- 2-3 Thai green chilies (adjust to taste)
- 1 shallot, chopped
- 3 cloves garlic, minced
- 1 thumb-sized piece of galangal or ginger, sliced
- 1 lemongrass stalk, thinly sliced (white part only)
- 1 kaffir lime peel (or use zest of 1 lime)
- 1 teaspoon ground coriander
- 1/2 teaspoon ground cumin
- 1/2 teaspoon shrimp paste (optional)
- 1/4 teaspoon white pepper
- 2 tablespoons cilantro stems, chopped
- 2 tablespoons vegetable oil

For Green Chicken Curry:

- 1 pound (450g) boneless, skinless chicken thighs, cut into bite-sized pieces
- 1 can (14 oz) coconut milk
- 2-3 tablespoons Green Curry Paste (from above)
- 1 cup eggplant, sliced
- 1 cup bamboo shoots, sliced (fresh or canned)
- 1 red bell pepper, sliced
- 1 tablespoon fish sauce
- 1 tablespoon soy sauce
- 1 tablespoon palm sugar or brown sugar
- Kaffir lime leaves, torn into pieces (optional)
- Thai basil leaves for garnish (optional)
- Cooked jasmine rice, for serving

Instructions:

For Green Curry Paste:

Prepare Ingredients:
Gather and prepare all the ingredients for the Green Curry Paste.

Blend:
In a food processor or blender, blend all the Green Curry Paste ingredients until you achieve a smooth and vibrant paste.

For Green Chicken Curry:

Cook Green Curry Paste:
In a large pot or wok, heat vegetable oil over medium heat. Add 2-3 tablespoons of the Green Curry Paste and stir-fry for 2-3 minutes until fragrant.

Add Coconut Milk:
Pour in the coconut milk and bring the mixture to a gentle simmer.

Add Chicken:
Add the bite-sized chicken pieces to the pot. Cook until the chicken is almost cooked through.

Add Vegetables:
Add sliced eggplant, bamboo shoots, and red bell pepper to the pot. Simmer until the vegetables are tender and the chicken is fully cooked.

Season:
Season the curry with fish sauce, soy sauce, and palm sugar. Stir well to combine.

Add Kaffir Lime Leaves (Optional):
If using kaffir lime leaves, add them to the curry for an additional layer of flavor.

Garnish:
Optionally, garnish the Green Chicken Curry with Thai basil leaves.

Serve:
Serve the Green Chicken Curry hot over cooked jasmine rice.

Enjoy the aromatic and flavorful Green Chicken Curry, a classic Thai dish that balances the richness of coconut milk with the freshness of herbs and spices. Adjust the level of spiciness and sweetness according to your preferences.

Khao Soi (Northern Thai Curry Noodles)

Ingredients:

For Khao Soi Paste:

- 2 shallots, chopped
- 4 cloves garlic, minced
- 1 thumb-sized piece of ginger, sliced
- 2-3 tablespoons red curry paste
- 1 tablespoon ground turmeric
- 1 tablespoon curry powder
- 1 teaspoon coriander powder
- 1 teaspoon cumin powder

For Khao Soi Curry:

- 2 tablespoons vegetable oil
- 1 can (14 oz) coconut milk
- 1-2 tablespoons Khao Soi paste (from above)
- 1 pound (450g) chicken thighs or beef, sliced
- 4 cups chicken or beef broth
- 2 tablespoons soy sauce
- 2 tablespoons fish sauce
- 1 tablespoon palm sugar or brown sugar
- Salt to taste

For Serving:

- Egg noodles, cooked
- Additional coconut milk (optional)
- Bean sprouts
- Fresh cilantro leaves
- Lime wedges
- Crispy fried noodles or shallots for garnish

Instructions:

For Khao Soi Paste:

Prepare Ingredients:
    Gather and prepare all the ingredients for the Khao Soi paste.

Blend:
: In a food processor or blender, blend all the Khao Soi paste ingredients until you achieve a smooth and vibrant paste.

For Khao Soi Curry:

Cook Khao Soi Paste:
: In a large pot, heat vegetable oil over medium heat. Add 1-2 tablespoons of the Khao Soi paste and sauté for 2-3 minutes until fragrant.

Add Coconut Milk:
: Pour in the coconut milk and bring the mixture to a gentle simmer.

Cook Chicken/Beef:
: Add the sliced chicken or beef to the pot. Cook until the meat is browned.

Add Broth:
: Pour in the chicken or beef broth and bring the soup to a simmer. Let it simmer for about 15-20 minutes.

Season:
: Season the Khao Soi curry with soy sauce, fish sauce, palm sugar, and salt to taste. Adjust the seasoning as needed.

Serve:
: Serve the Khao Soi hot over cooked egg noodles.

For Serving:

Garnish and Serve:
- Top the Khao Soi with bean sprouts, fresh cilantro leaves, and lime wedges.
- Optionally, drizzle with additional coconut milk for extra creaminess.
- Garnish with crispy fried noodles or shallots for added crunch.

Enjoy the rich and flavorful taste of homemade Khao Soi, a Northern Thai curry noodle soup that combines the creaminess of coconut milk with the bold flavors of herbs and spices. Adjust the spice level and toppings according to your preferences.

Pad Prik Khing (Stir-Fried Red Curry Paste)

Ingredients:

For Prik Khing Paste:

- 5-6 dried red chili peppers, soaked in warm water
- 2 tablespoons chopped shallots
- 3 cloves garlic
- 1 teaspoon galangal or ginger, sliced
- 1 lemongrass stalk, thinly sliced (white part only)
- 1 kaffir lime peel or lime zest
- 1 teaspoon ground coriander
- 1/2 teaspoon cumin
- 1/2 teaspoon shrimp paste (optional)
- 2 tablespoons vegetable oil

For Stir-Fry:

- 1 pound (450g) protein of choice (chicken, beef, pork, tofu), thinly sliced
- 2 tablespoons Prik Khing paste (from above)
- 1 cup green beans, trimmed and cut into bite-sized pieces
- 2 kaffir lime leaves, finely shredded (optional)
- 2 tablespoons fish sauce
- 1 tablespoon soy sauce
- 1 tablespoon palm sugar or brown sugar
- 1 tablespoon vegetable oil
- Fresh Thai basil leaves for garnish (optional)
- Cooked jasmine rice, for serving

Instructions:

For Prik Khing Paste:

Prepare Ingredients:
    Gather and prepare all the ingredients for the Prik Khing paste.

Blend:
    In a food processor or blender, blend all the Prik Khing paste ingredients until you achieve a smooth paste.

For Stir-Fry:

Cook Protein:
Heat vegetable oil in a wok or a large skillet over medium-high heat. Add the sliced protein (chicken, beef, pork, tofu) and cook until browned and fully cooked. Remove from the wok and set aside.

Stir-Fry Beans:
In the same wok, add a bit more oil if needed. Add the green beans and stir-fry until they are slightly tender but still crisp.

Add Prik Khing Paste:
Push the beans to one side of the wok and add 2 tablespoons of the Prik Khing paste to the other side. Stir-fry the paste for about 1-2 minutes until fragrant.

Combine Ingredients:
Mix the cooked protein back into the wok with the stir-fried beans and Prik Khing paste.

Season:
Season the stir-fry with fish sauce, soy sauce, and palm sugar. Stir well to combine.

Add Kaffir Lime Leaves (Optional):
If using kaffir lime leaves, add them to the wok for an additional layer of flavor.

Garnish and Serve:
Optionally, garnish the Pad Prik Khing with fresh Thai basil leaves. Serve the stir-fry hot over cooked jasmine rice.

Enjoy the bold and spicy flavors of Pad Prik Khing, a quick and flavorful Thai stir-fry that showcases the aromatic red curry paste. Adjust the level of spiciness and sweetness according to your preferences.

Moo Pad Krapow (Stir-Fried Pork with Basil)

Ingredients:

- 1 pound (450g) ground pork
- 2 tablespoons vegetable oil
- 4 cloves garlic, minced
- 2-3 Thai bird's eye chilies, chopped (adjust to taste)
- 1 cup fresh Thai basil leaves
- 1 red bell pepper, sliced
- 1 onion, sliced
- 2 tablespoons oyster sauce
- 1 tablespoon soy sauce
- 1 teaspoon fish sauce
- 1 teaspoon sugar
- Freshly ground black pepper, to taste
- Jasmine rice, for serving
- Fried or sunny-side-up eggs, for serving (optional)

Instructions:

Prepare Ingredients:
- Gather and prepare all the ingredients for Moo Pad Krapow.

Stir-Fry Pork:
- In a wok or large skillet, heat vegetable oil over medium-high heat.
- Add minced garlic and chopped Thai chilies. Stir-fry for about 30 seconds until fragrant.

Cook Ground Pork:
- Add ground pork to the wok. Break it up and cook until browned and fully cooked.

Add Vegetables:
- Add sliced red bell pepper and onion to the wok. Stir-fry until the vegetables are tender-crisp.

Season:
- In a small bowl, mix oyster sauce, soy sauce, fish sauce, sugar, and black pepper.
- Pour the sauce over the pork and vegetables. Stir well to combine.

Add Thai Basil:
- Add fresh Thai basil leaves to the wok. Stir-fry for a minute until the basil wilts and releases its aroma.

Taste and Adjust:
- Taste the Moo Pad Krapow and adjust the seasoning if needed. You can add more soy sauce, fish sauce, or sugar according to your taste.

Serve:
- Serve the Moo Pad Krapow hot over jasmine rice.
- Optionally, top with a fried or sunny-side-up egg.

Enjoy the bold and savory flavors of Moo Pad Krapow, a quick and delicious Thai stir-fry that's perfect for a satisfying meal. Adjust the level of spiciness by varying the amount of Thai chilies.

Drunken Noodles (Pad Kee Mao)

Ingredients:

- 8 oz (about 225g) wide rice noodles
- 2 tablespoons vegetable oil
- 3 cloves garlic, minced
- 2 Thai bird's eye chilies, chopped (adjust to taste)
- 1/2 pound (225g) protein of choice (chicken, beef, shrimp, tofu), sliced
- 1 cup bell peppers, sliced (use a mix of colors)
- 1 cup broccoli florets
- 2 tablespoons oyster sauce
- 1 tablespoon soy sauce
- 1 tablespoon fish sauce
- 1 teaspoon sugar
- Fresh basil leaves, for garnish
- Lime wedges, for serving

Instructions:

Prepare Noodles:
- Cook the wide rice noodles according to package instructions. Drain and set aside.

Stir-Fry:
- Heat vegetable oil in a wok or large skillet over medium-high heat.
- Add minced garlic and chopped Thai chilies. Stir-fry for about 30 seconds until fragrant.

Cook Protein:
- Add the sliced protein (chicken, beef, shrimp, tofu) to the wok. Cook until browned and fully cooked.

Add Vegetables:
- Add sliced bell peppers and broccoli florets to the wok. Stir-fry until the vegetables are tender-crisp.

Season:
- In a small bowl, mix oyster sauce, soy sauce, fish sauce, and sugar.
- Pour the sauce over the noodles and vegetables. Toss everything together until well combined.

Add Noodles:
- Add the cooked rice noodles to the wok. Toss and stir-fry until the noodles are evenly coated with the sauce and heated through.

Garnish:
- Garnish the Drunken Noodles with fresh basil leaves.

Serve:
- Serve the Drunken Noodles hot, garnished with lime wedges on the side.

Enjoy the bold and spicy flavors of homemade Drunken Noodles. Adjust the level of spiciness by varying the amount of Thai chilies. This dish is versatile, allowing you to customize the protein and vegetables based on your preferences.

Yum Woon Sen (Glass Noodle Salad)

Ingredients:

For Glass Noodle Salad:

- 100g (3.5 oz) dried glass noodles (bean thread noodles)
- 200g (about 7 oz) cooked and peeled shrimp, or tofu for a vegetarian version
- 1 cup cherry tomatoes, halved
- 1 cup cucumber, thinly sliced
- 1/2 cup red onion, thinly sliced
- 1/4 cup cilantro, chopped
- 1/4 cup green onions, sliced
- 1/4 cup roasted peanuts, crushed
- Fresh lettuce leaves for serving

For Dressing:

- 3 tablespoons fish sauce (or soy sauce for a vegetarian version)
- 2 tablespoons lime juice
- 1 tablespoon palm sugar or brown sugar
- 1-2 Thai bird's eye chilies, finely chopped (adjust to taste)
- 2 cloves garlic, minced

Instructions:

Prepare Glass Noodles:
- Soak the dried glass noodles in hot water for about 5-7 minutes or until they are soft and transparent. Drain and set aside.

Cook Protein (Shrimp or Tofu):
- If using shrimp, cook them in boiling water for 2-3 minutes or until they turn pink and opaque. If using tofu, pan-fry or grill until lightly browned. Set aside.

Prepare Vegetables:
- In a large bowl, combine cherry tomatoes, cucumber, red onion, cilantro, and green onions.

Assemble Salad:
- Add the soaked glass noodles to the bowl with vegetables. Toss everything together.

Prepare Dressing:

- In a small bowl, whisk together fish sauce, lime juice, palm sugar, chopped Thai chilies, and minced garlic until the sugar dissolves.

Dress Salad:
- Pour the dressing over the glass noodle and vegetable mixture. Toss to coat everything evenly.

Add Protein and Peanuts:
- Add the cooked shrimp or tofu to the salad. Toss gently.

Garnish:
- Sprinkle crushed roasted peanuts over the top.

Serve:
- Serve the Yum Woon Sen on a bed of fresh lettuce leaves.

Enjoy the light and vibrant flavors of Yum Woon Sen, a delightful Thai Glass Noodle Salad. Adjust the level of spiciness in the dressing according to your preference.

Grilled Lemongrass Chicken

Ingredients:

For Lemongrass Chicken Marinade:

- 1.5 pounds (about 700g) boneless, skinless chicken thighs, cut into bite-sized pieces
- 3 stalks lemongrass, white part only, finely minced
- 3 cloves garlic, minced
- 1 tablespoon fresh ginger, grated
- 2 tablespoons soy sauce
- 1 tablespoon fish sauce
- 1 tablespoon oyster sauce
- 1 tablespoon honey or brown sugar
- 1 tablespoon vegetable oil
- 1 teaspoon ground coriander
- 1 teaspoon ground turmeric
- 1 teaspoon paprika (optional, for color)
- Freshly ground black pepper, to taste

For Serving:

- Fresh cilantro, chopped
- Lime wedges
- Thai sweet chili sauce (optional)

Instructions:

Prepare Lemongrass:
- Trim the tough outer layers of the lemongrass stalks. Finely mince the white part.

Make Marinade:
- In a bowl, combine minced lemongrass, minced garlic, grated ginger, soy sauce, fish sauce, oyster sauce, honey or brown sugar, vegetable oil, ground coriander, ground turmeric, paprika (if using), and freshly ground black pepper.

Marinate Chicken:
- Add the bite-sized chicken pieces to the marinade. Ensure the chicken is well-coated. Cover and refrigerate for at least 1-2 hours, or overnight for better flavor.

Preheat Grill:

- Preheat your grill to medium-high heat.

Skewer Chicken:
- Thread the marinated chicken pieces onto skewers.

Grill Chicken:
- Grill the lemongrass chicken skewers for about 5-7 minutes per side or until fully cooked and charred.

Serve:
- Remove the chicken skewers from the grill and transfer them to a serving plate.
- Garnish with chopped fresh cilantro and serve with lime wedges.
- Optionally, serve with Thai sweet chili sauce on the side for dipping.

Enjoy:
- Enjoy the Grilled Lemongrass Chicken hot, either on its own or with rice.

This Grilled Lemongrass Chicken is a delightful combination of savory, sweet, and aromatic flavors. The lemongrass adds a refreshing and citrusy note to the dish. Adjust the level of sweetness and spiciness according to your preference.

Thai Basil Fried Rice

Ingredients:

- 3 cups cooked jasmine rice (preferably day-old and chilled)
- 2 tablespoons vegetable oil
- 3 cloves garlic, minced
- 1-2 Thai bird's eye chilies, chopped (adjust to taste)
- 1 cup protein of choice (chicken, beef, shrimp, tofu), diced
- 1 cup bell peppers, diced (use a mix of colors)
- 1 cup green beans, chopped
- 1 tablespoon oyster sauce
- 1 tablespoon soy sauce
- 1 teaspoon fish sauce
- 1 teaspoon sugar
- 1 cup fresh Thai basil leaves
- Fried or sunny-side-up eggs, for serving (optional)
- Sliced cucumber and lime wedges, for garnish

Instructions:

Prepare Ingredients:
- Ensure that all the ingredients are chopped and ready before you start cooking.

Heat Oil:
- Heat vegetable oil in a wok or large skillet over medium-high heat.

Sauté Garlic and Chilies:
- Add minced garlic and chopped Thai chilies to the hot oil. Sauté for about 30 seconds until fragrant.

Add Protein:
- Add the diced protein (chicken, beef, shrimp, tofu) to the wok. Cook until browned and fully cooked.

Stir-Fry Vegetables:
- Add diced bell peppers and chopped green beans to the wok. Stir-fry for 2-3 minutes until the vegetables are tender-crisp.

Season with Sauces:
- In a small bowl, mix oyster sauce, soy sauce, fish sauce, and sugar. Pour the sauce over the ingredients in the wok.

Add Rice:

- Add the chilled cooked jasmine rice to the wok. Use a spatula to break up any clumps and stir the rice evenly with the other ingredients.

Incorporate Basil:
- Add fresh Thai basil leaves to the wok. Stir until the basil wilts and releases its aroma.

Taste and Adjust:
- Taste the fried rice and adjust the seasoning if needed. You can add more soy sauce, fish sauce, or sugar according to your taste.

Serve:
- Optionally, serve Thai Basil Fried Rice with fried or sunny-side-up eggs on top.
- Garnish with sliced cucumber and lime wedges on the side.

Enjoy:
- Enjoy the Thai Basil Fried Rice hot, savoring the aromatic blend of basil and savory flavors.

This Thai Basil Fried Rice is a quick and flavorful dish that can be customized with your choice of protein. Adjust the level of spiciness and add more basil for a burst of fresh and aromatic taste.

Thai Red Curry Shrimp

Ingredients:

For Red Curry Paste:

- 2 tablespoons red curry paste
- 2 tablespoons vegetable oil
- 1 teaspoon ground coriander
- 1 teaspoon ground cumin
- 1 teaspoon paprika
- 1/2 teaspoon cayenne pepper (adjust to taste)

For Thai Red Curry Shrimp:

- 1 pound (450g) large shrimp, peeled and deveined
- 1 can (14 oz) coconut milk
- 1 red bell pepper, sliced
- 1 cup bamboo shoots, sliced (fresh or canned)
- 1 cup snap peas, ends trimmed
- 1 tablespoon fish sauce
- 1 tablespoon soy sauce
- 1 tablespoon palm sugar or brown sugar
- Fresh Thai basil leaves for garnish
- Cooked jasmine rice, for serving

Instructions:

For Red Curry Paste:

Prepare Ingredients:
- Gather and prepare all the ingredients for the red curry paste.

Make Red Curry Paste:
- In a small bowl, mix red curry paste, vegetable oil, ground coriander, ground cumin, paprika, and cayenne pepper. Set aside.

For Thai Red Curry Shrimp:

Cook Red Curry Paste:
- In a wok or large skillet, heat the red curry paste mixture over medium heat. Stir and cook for 1-2 minutes until fragrant.

Add Coconut Milk:
- Pour in the coconut milk, stirring to combine with the red curry paste. Bring the mixture to a gentle simmer.

Add Shrimp:
- Add the peeled and deveined shrimp to the wok. Cook until the shrimp turn pink and opaque.

Add Vegetables:
- Add sliced red bell pepper, bamboo shoots, and snap peas to the wok. Simmer until the vegetables are tender-crisp.

Season:
- Season the Thai Red Curry Shrimp with fish sauce, soy sauce, and palm sugar. Stir well to combine.

Simmer:
- Let the curry simmer for a few more minutes until the flavors meld together.

Garnish:
- Garnish the Thai Red Curry Shrimp with fresh Thai basil leaves.

Serve:
- Serve the Thai Red Curry Shrimp hot over cooked jasmine rice.

Enjoy the delicious and aromatic Thai Red Curry Shrimp, a perfect balance of spicy, savory, and creamy flavors. Customize the level of spiciness by adjusting the amount of red curry paste and cayenne pepper to suit your taste.

Nam Prik Ong (Northern Thai Chili Dip)

Ingredients:

- 200g ground pork
- 1 cup tomatoes, diced
- 3-4 shallots, finely chopped
- 4 cloves garlic, minced
- 2-3 Thai bird's eye chilies, finely chopped (adjust to taste)
- 1 tablespoon vegetable oil
- 1 tablespoon shrimp paste
- 1 teaspoon ground coriander
- 1 teaspoon ground cumin
- 1 teaspoon paprika
- 1/2 teaspoon turmeric powder
- 1/2 cup chicken or pork broth
- 1 tablespoon fish sauce
- 1 teaspoon sugar
- Fresh cilantro leaves for garnish
- Fresh vegetables (cucumber, long beans, etc.) for serving

Instructions:

Prepare Ingredients:
- Gather and prepare all the ingredients for Nam Prik Ong.

Cook Ground Pork:
- In a pan, heat vegetable oil over medium heat. Add ground pork and cook until browned.

Add Aromatics:
- Add shallots, garlic, and Thai bird's eye chilies to the pan. Cook until the aromatics are fragrant.

Add Spices and Shrimp Paste:
- Stir in shrimp paste, ground coriander, ground cumin, paprika, and turmeric powder. Mix well with the pork mixture.

Add Tomatoes:
- Add diced tomatoes to the pan and cook until they release their juices.

Simmer:
- Pour in chicken or pork broth and let the mixture simmer for about 10-15 minutes until it thickens.

Season:

- Season Nam Prik Ong with fish sauce and sugar. Adjust the seasoning to your taste.

Garnish:
- Garnish with fresh cilantro leaves.

Serve:
- Serve Nam Prik Ong hot with fresh vegetables on the side.

Enjoy Nam Prik Ong, a savory and slightly spicy Northern Thai chili dip that perfectly complements fresh vegetables or steamed rice. Adjust the level of spiciness by varying the amount of Thai bird's eye chilies.

Pla Rad Prik (Fried Fish with Chili Sauce)

Ingredients:

For Fried Fish:

- 2 whole fish (such as tilapia or snapper), cleaned and scaled
- Salt and pepper, to taste
- Cornstarch, for dusting
- Vegetable oil, for frying

For Chili Sauce:

- 3 tablespoons vegetable oil
- 3 cloves garlic, minced
- 2-3 Thai bird's eye chilies, finely chopped (adjust to taste)
- 1/4 cup shallots, thinly sliced
- 1/4 cup bell peppers (red and green), thinly sliced
- 1/4 cup carrots, julienned
- 3 tablespoons fish sauce
- 1 tablespoon soy sauce
- 1 tablespoon oyster sauce
- 1 tablespoon sugar
- 1 tablespoon water
- Fresh cilantro leaves for garnish
- Sliced green onions for garnish
- Lime wedges for serving

Instructions:

For Fried Fish:

Prepare Fish:
- Pat the fish dry with paper towels. Score both sides of the fish with shallow cuts. Season with salt and pepper.

Dust with Cornstarch:
- Lightly dust the fish with cornstarch, shaking off any excess.

Fry Fish:
- In a large pan, heat vegetable oil over medium-high heat. Fry the fish until golden brown and crispy on both sides. Drain on paper towels.

For Chili Sauce:

Make Chili Sauce:
- In a separate pan, heat vegetable oil over medium heat. Add minced garlic and chopped Thai bird's eye chilies. Sauté until fragrant.

Add Vegetables:
- Add sliced shallots, bell peppers, and julienned carrots to the pan. Stir-fry until the vegetables are slightly softened.

Prepare Sauce:
- In a bowl, mix fish sauce, soy sauce, oyster sauce, sugar, and water. Pour the sauce into the pan with the vegetables. Stir well to combine.

Simmer:
- Let the sauce simmer for a few minutes until it thickens slightly.

Assemble:
- Place the fried fish on a serving platter. Pour the chili sauce over the top.

Garnish:
- Garnish Pla Rad Prik with fresh cilantro leaves and sliced green onions.

Serve:
- Serve the Fried Fish with Chili Sauce hot, with lime wedges on the side.

Enjoy the crispy texture of the fried fish combined with the bold and spicy flavors of the chili sauce. Pla Rad Prik is a delightful Thai dish that offers a perfect balance of textures and tastes. Adjust the level of spiciness to your liking.

Panang Moo Tod (Panang Curry Pork)

Ingredients:

For Panang Curry Paste:

- 2 tablespoons Panang curry paste
- 1 tablespoon vegetable oil
- 2 tablespoons chopped shallots
- 3 cloves garlic, minced
- 1 teaspoon ground coriander
- 1 teaspoon ground cumin
- 1/2 teaspoon shrimp paste (optional)
- 1/2 teaspoon salt

For Panang Curry Pork:

- 1 pound (450g) pork tenderloin or pork shoulder, thinly sliced
- 1 can (14 oz) coconut milk
- 2 tablespoons fish sauce
- 1 tablespoon soy sauce
- 1 tablespoon palm sugar or brown sugar
- 1 kaffir lime leaf, finely shredded (optional)
- 1 red chili, sliced (for garnish)
- Fresh Thai basil leaves for garnish
- Cooked jasmine rice, for serving

Instructions:

For Panang Curry Paste:

Prepare Ingredients:
- Gather and prepare all the ingredients for the Panang curry paste.

Make Panang Curry Paste:
- In a mortar and pestle or a food processor, grind or blend together Panang curry paste ingredients until you get a smooth paste.

For Panang Curry Pork:

Cook Panang Curry Paste:

- In a wok or a large skillet, heat vegetable oil over medium heat. Add the Panang curry paste and cook for 2-3 minutes until fragrant.

Add Pork:
- Add the thinly sliced pork to the wok. Stir-fry until the pork is cooked through.

Add Coconut Milk:
- Pour in the coconut milk and bring the mixture to a gentle simmer.

Season:
- Season the Panang Curry Pork with fish sauce, soy sauce, and palm sugar. Stir well to combine.

Simmer:
- Let the curry simmer for about 10-15 minutes until the flavors meld together, and the sauce thickens.

Add Kaffir Lime Leaf (Optional):
- If using kaffir lime leaf, add the finely shredded leaf to the curry for an additional layer of flavor.

Garnish:
- Garnish the Panang Curry Pork with sliced red chili and fresh Thai basil leaves.

Serve:
- Serve the Panang Moo Tod hot over cooked jasmine rice.

Enjoy the rich and aromatic flavors of Panang Moo Tod, a Thai curry dish that combines the creaminess of coconut milk with the bold and complex taste of Panang curry paste. Adjust the level of spiciness and sweetness according to your preferences.

Thai Crab Fried Rice

Ingredients:

- 2 cups cooked jasmine rice (preferably day-old and chilled)
- 200g crab meat (fresh or canned), picked and cleaned
- 2 tablespoons vegetable oil
- 3 cloves garlic, minced
- 2 eggs, beaten
- 1 cup mixed vegetables (peas, carrots, corn), thawed if frozen
- 3 green onions, chopped
- 1 tablespoon fish sauce
- 1 tablespoon soy sauce
- 1 teaspoon oyster sauce
- 1 teaspoon sugar
- 1/2 teaspoon white pepper
- Fresh cilantro leaves for garnish
- Lime wedges for serving

Instructions:

Prepare Ingredients:
- Gather and prepare all the ingredients for Thai Crab Fried Rice.

Heat Oil:
- Heat vegetable oil in a wok or large skillet over medium-high heat.

Sauté Garlic:
- Add minced garlic to the hot oil and sauté until fragrant.

Add Crab Meat:
- Add the cleaned crab meat to the wok. Stir-fry for 2-3 minutes until heated through.

Push Ingredients to the Side:
- Push the crab meat to one side of the wok, creating space for the eggs.

Scramble Eggs:
- Pour beaten eggs into the empty side of the wok. Scramble the eggs until they are just set.

Mix In Vegetables:
- Combine the scrambled eggs with the crab meat. Add mixed vegetables and chopped green onions. Stir-fry for an additional 2-3 minutes.

Add Rice:

- Add the chilled cooked jasmine rice to the wok. Use a spatula to break up any clumps and mix the rice evenly with the other ingredients.

Season:
- Season the Thai Crab Fried Rice with fish sauce, soy sauce, oyster sauce, sugar, and white pepper. Stir well to combine.

Garnish:
- Garnish the fried rice with fresh cilantro leaves.

Serve:
- Serve Thai Crab Fried Rice hot, with lime wedges on the side.

Enjoy the delightful flavors of Thai Crab Fried Rice, a dish that balances the sweetness of crab meat with savory and aromatic seasonings. Adjust the seasoning according to your taste preferences.

Green Papaya Soup with Pork Ribs

Ingredients:

For the Broth:

- 1 pound pork ribs
- 1 onion, quartered
- 2-3 cloves garlic, smashed
- 1 thumb-sized piece of ginger, sliced
- 1 lemongrass stalk, smashed
- 2-3 kaffir lime leaves
- 8 cups water

For the Soup:

- 1 small green papaya, peeled, seeds removed, and thinly sliced
- 1 cup cherry tomatoes, halved
- 1 cup baby bok choy or spinach, chopped
- 2 tablespoons fish sauce
- 1 tablespoon soy sauce
- 1 tablespoon lime juice
- 1 teaspoon sugar
- Fresh cilantro leaves for garnish
- Thai bird's eye chilies, sliced (optional, for extra heat)

Instructions:

For the Broth:

Prepare Pork Ribs:
- Rinse the pork ribs under cold water and set aside.

Boil Broth:
- In a large pot, bring 8 cups of water to a boil. Add the pork ribs, quartered onion, smashed garlic, sliced ginger, smashed lemongrass stalk, and kaffir lime leaves.

Simmer:
- Reduce heat to low, cover the pot, and let it simmer for about 1 to 1.5 hours until the pork ribs are tender and flavorful.

Strain Broth:
- Strain the broth to remove the solids, leaving only the clear broth. Discard the solids.

For the Soup:

- Prepare Ingredients:
  - Slice the green papaya, halve the cherry tomatoes, chop the baby bok choy or spinach, and set aside.
- Add Vegetables:
  - Bring the strained broth back to a simmer. Add the sliced green papaya, halved cherry tomatoes, and chopped bok choy or spinach.
- Season:
  - Season the soup with fish sauce, soy sauce, lime juice, and sugar. Adjust the seasoning to your taste.
- Simmer:
  - Let the soup simmer for an additional 10-15 minutes until the vegetables are tender.
- Taste and Adjust:
  - Taste the soup and adjust the seasoning if needed. Add more fish sauce, soy sauce, or lime juice according to your preference.
- Serve:
  - Ladle the Green Papaya Soup with Pork Ribs into bowls. Garnish with fresh cilantro leaves and sliced Thai bird's eye chilies if you like it spicy.

Enjoy this comforting and nutritious Green Papaya Soup with Pork Ribs, filled with the freshness of green papaya and the savory goodness of pork ribs. Adjust the level of spiciness and acidity to suit your taste.

Pad Cha Talay (Seafood Stir-Fry)

Ingredients:

For the Stir-Fry:

- 200g shrimp, peeled and deveined
- 200g squid, cleaned and sliced into rings
- 200g mussels, cleaned and debearded
- 200g firm white fish fillets, cut into bite-sized pieces
- 1 cup mixed vegetables (bell peppers, baby corn, Thai eggplant, bamboo shoots), sliced
- 2 tablespoons vegetable oil

For the Curry Paste:

- 2 tablespoons red curry paste
- 1 tablespoon green peppercorns, crushed
- 1 tablespoon fresh green peppercorns (optional)
- 1 tablespoon galangal, sliced
- 1 tablespoon lemongrass, sliced
- 4 kaffir lime leaves, torn
- 1 Thai bird's eye chili, chopped (adjust to taste)
- 3 cloves garlic, minced

For the Sauce:

- 2 tablespoons fish sauce
- 1 tablespoon oyster sauce
- 1 tablespoon soy sauce
- 1 teaspoon sugar

For Garnish:

- Fresh Thai basil leaves
- Fresh cilantro leaves
- Sliced red chili (for extra heat)

Instructions:

Prepare Ingredients:
- Clean and prepare all seafood and vegetables.

Make Curry Paste:

- In a mortar and pestle or a food processor, grind or blend together all the curry paste ingredients until you get a smooth paste.

Prepare Sauce:
- In a small bowl, mix together fish sauce, oyster sauce, soy sauce, and sugar.

Stir-Fry:
- Heat vegetable oil in a wok or a large skillet over medium-high heat. Add the curry paste and stir-fry for 1-2 minutes until fragrant.

Add Seafood:
- Add shrimp, squid, mussels, and fish to the wok. Stir-fry for 2-3 minutes until the seafood starts to cook.

Add Vegetables:
- Add the mixed vegetables to the wok. Stir-fry for an additional 2-3 minutes until the vegetables are tender-crisp.

Pour Sauce:
- Pour the prepared sauce over the seafood and vegetables. Stir well to combine.

Add Fresh Peppercorns:
- If using fresh green peppercorns, add them to the wok and stir-fry for an additional minute.

Garnish:
- Garnish Pad Cha Talay with fresh Thai basil leaves, cilantro leaves, and sliced red chili for extra heat.

Serve:
- Serve the Pad Cha Talay hot over steamed jasmine rice.

Enjoy the bold and spicy flavors of Pad Cha Talay, a delicious Thai seafood stir-fry that highlights the aromatic blend of herbs and spices. Adjust the level of spiciness by varying the amount of Thai bird's eye chili.

Pad Ped Moo (Spicy Stir-Fried Pork)

Ingredients:

For the Curry Paste:

- 2 tablespoons red curry paste
- 1 tablespoon green peppercorns, crushed
- 1 tablespoon galangal, sliced
- 1 tablespoon lemongrass, sliced
- 4 kaffir lime leaves, torn
- 1 Thai bird's eye chili, chopped (adjust to taste)
- 3 cloves garlic, minced

For the Stir-Fry:

- 500g pork loin or pork shoulder, thinly sliced
- 2 tablespoons vegetable oil
- 1 cup Thai eggplants, halved
- 1 cup bamboo shoots, sliced
- 1 red bell pepper, sliced
- 1 cup coconut milk
- 2 tablespoons fish sauce
- 1 tablespoon soy sauce
- 1 tablespoon oyster sauce
- 1 teaspoon sugar

For Garnish:

- Fresh Thai basil leaves
- Fresh cilantro leaves
- Sliced red chili (for extra heat)

Instructions:

For the Curry Paste:

Prepare Ingredients:
- Gather and prepare all the ingredients for the curry paste.

Make Curry Paste:
- In a mortar and pestle or a food processor, grind or blend together all the curry paste ingredients until you get a smooth paste.

For the Stir-Fry:

- Prepare Pork:
  - Thinly slice the pork loin or pork shoulder and set aside.
- Stir-Fry Curry Paste:
  - Heat vegetable oil in a wok or a large skillet over medium-high heat. Add the prepared curry paste and stir-fry for 1-2 minutes until fragrant.
- Add Pork:
  - Add the sliced pork to the wok. Stir-fry for 3-4 minutes until the pork is cooked and coated with the curry paste.
- Add Vegetables:
  - Add Thai eggplants, bamboo shoots, and sliced red bell pepper to the wok. Stir-fry for an additional 2-3 minutes until the vegetables are tender-crisp.
- Pour Coconut Milk:
  - Pour coconut milk into the wok and stir well.
- Season:
  - Season the stir-fry with fish sauce, soy sauce, oyster sauce, and sugar. Stir to combine.
- Simmer:
  - Let the Pad Ped Moo simmer for 5-7 minutes until the flavors meld together and the sauce thickens slightly.
- Garnish:
  - Garnish with fresh Thai basil leaves, cilantro leaves, and sliced red chili.
- Serve:
  - Serve Pad Ped Moo hot over steamed jasmine rice.

Enjoy the bold and spicy flavors of Pad Ped Moo, a delicious Thai stir-fried pork dish. Adjust the level of spiciness according to your taste preference.

Nam Tok Moo (Grilled Pork Salad)

Ingredients:

For the Grilled Pork:

- 500g pork loin or pork shoulder, thinly sliced
- 2 tablespoons soy sauce
- 1 tablespoon oyster sauce
- 1 tablespoon fish sauce
- 1 tablespoon sugar
- 1 teaspoon black pepper

For the Salad:

- 1 cup thinly sliced shallots
- 1 cup chopped green onions
- 1 cup fresh cilantro, chopped
- 1 cup mint leaves, torn
- 1-2 tablespoons roasted rice powder (ground toasted rice)

For the Dressing:

- 3 tablespoons fish sauce
- 2 tablespoons lime juice
- 1 tablespoon sugar
- 1-2 teaspoons chili flakes (adjust to taste)

Instructions:

In a bowl, mix the soy sauce, oyster sauce, fish sauce, sugar, and black pepper to create a marinade for the pork.

Add the thinly sliced pork to the marinade, ensuring each slice is well-coated. Let it marinate for at least 30 minutes to allow the flavors to infuse.

While the pork is marinating, prepare the dressing by combining fish sauce, lime juice, sugar, and chili flakes in a separate bowl. Adjust the seasoning according to your taste preferences.

Preheat the grill or a grill pan over medium-high heat. Grill the marinated pork slices until they are cooked through and have a nice char, usually 2-3 minutes per side.

Once the pork is grilled, let it rest for a few minutes, then thinly slice it into bite-sized pieces.

In a large mixing bowl, combine the grilled pork with sliced shallots, chopped green onions, cilantro, and torn mint leaves.

Pour the dressing over the salad and toss everything together until well combined.

Sprinkle roasted rice powder over the top for added texture and flavor.

Serve the Nam Tok Moo immediately, either as a main dish or as part of a Thai meal with rice on the side.

Nam Tok Moo is known for its bold and refreshing flavors, combining the savory grilled pork with the vibrant herbs and zesty dressing. Adjust the spice level and seasonings to suit your taste preferences. Enjoy!

Pla Tod Kamin (Turmeric Fried Fish)

Ingredients:

- 2 whole fish (such as tilapia or sea bass), cleaned and scaled
- 2 tablespoons turmeric powder
- 1 teaspoon salt
- 1 teaspoon black pepper
- 1 tablespoon fish sauce
- 2 tablespoons oyster sauce
- 2 tablespoons light soy sauce
- 1 tablespoon sugar
- Vegetable oil for deep frying

For Garnish (optional):

- Fresh cilantro, chopped
- Thinly sliced red chili

Instructions:

Clean and scale the whole fish, making sure they are thoroughly dry. You can ask your fishmonger to do this for you.
In a bowl, mix turmeric powder, salt, black pepper, fish sauce, oyster sauce, light soy sauce, and sugar to create a marinade.
Rub the marinade all over the fish, making sure to coat both sides and inside the cavity. Allow the fish to marinate for at least 30 minutes to let the flavors infuse.
Heat vegetable oil in a deep fryer or a large, deep pan to 350-375°F (175-190°C). Carefully place the marinated fish in the hot oil, one at a time, ensuring not to overcrowd the pan. Fry the fish until they are golden brown and crispy, turning once to cook both sides evenly. This usually takes about 6-8 minutes per side, depending on the size of the fish.
Once the fish is cooked, use a slotted spoon to remove them from the oil and place them on a plate lined with paper towels to absorb any excess oil.
Garnish the fried fish with chopped cilantro and thinly sliced red chili if desired. Serve the Pla Tod Kamin hot with steamed rice and your favorite dipping sauce, such as sweet chili sauce or a traditional Thai dipping sauce made with fish sauce, lime juice, sugar, and chopped chili.

Enjoy the crispy and flavorful goodness of Pla Tod Kamin as a main dish in your Thai meal!

Thai Coconut Ice Cream

Ingredients:

- 2 cans (800ml) coconut milk
- 1 cup sugar
- 1/2 teaspoon salt
- 1 teaspoon vanilla extract
- 2 cups shredded coconut (optional, for added texture)
- Ice cream maker

Instructions:

In a saucepan over medium heat, combine the coconut milk, sugar, and salt. Stir continuously until the sugar dissolves and the mixture is well combined. Be careful not to let it come to a boil.
Remove the mixture from heat and let it cool to room temperature.
Once the mixture has cooled, add vanilla extract and stir well.
If you want to add texture to your coconut ice cream, you can toast the shredded coconut in a dry pan over medium heat until it turns golden brown. Allow it to cool.
Combine the cooled coconut milk mixture with the toasted shredded coconut (if using).
Transfer the mixture to the refrigerator and let it chill for at least 2-4 hours or overnight.
Once the mixture is thoroughly chilled, pour it into your ice cream maker and churn according to the manufacturer's instructions until it reaches a soft-serve consistency.
If you don't have an ice cream maker, you can pour the mixture into a shallow dish and freeze it. Every 30 minutes, take it out and stir vigorously with a fork to break up any ice crystals. Repeat this process 3-4 times until the ice cream reaches the desired consistency.
Once the ice cream is ready, transfer it to a lidded container and freeze for an additional 2 hours or until firm.
Scoop the Thai Coconut Ice Cream into bowls or cones, and garnish with additional shredded coconut if desired.

Enjoy the tropical flavors of homemade Thai Coconut Ice Cream on a hot day or as a delightful dessert after a Thai-inspired meal!

Pad Ma Kuer Yao (Stir-Fried Eggplant)

Ingredients:

- 2 medium-sized Asian eggplants or 1 large eggplant, cut into bite-sized pieces
- 2 tablespoons vegetable oil
- 3 cloves garlic, minced
- 1 red chili, thinly sliced (adjust according to spice preference)
- 1 tablespoon oyster sauce
- 1 tablespoon soy sauce
- 1 teaspoon sugar
- 1 tablespoon fish sauce
- 1/2 cup Thai basil leaves (holy basil), or regular basil as a substitute
- Spring onions (scallions), chopped, for garnish (optional)

Instructions:

Prepare the eggplant by cutting it into bite-sized pieces. If you're using Asian eggplants, you can cut them into rounds or wedges.

In a wok or a large skillet, heat the vegetable oil over medium-high heat.

Add minced garlic and sliced red chili to the hot oil. Stir-fry for about 30 seconds until fragrant.

Add the eggplant to the wok and stir-fry for 3-5 minutes until the pieces are slightly tender and starting to brown.

In a small bowl, mix together the oyster sauce, soy sauce, sugar, and fish sauce to create the stir-fry sauce.

Pour the sauce over the eggplant and continue to stir-fry for an additional 2-3 minutes, ensuring that the eggplant is well-coated with the sauce.

Add Thai basil leaves to the wok and stir-fry for an additional 1-2 minutes until the basil wilts and releases its aroma.

Taste and adjust the seasoning if needed, adding more soy sauce, fish sauce, or sugar according to your preference.

Once the eggplant is cooked through and well-coated with the sauce, remove the wok from heat.

Garnish with chopped spring onions if desired.

Serve Pad Ma Kuer Yao over steamed rice as a flavorful and vegetarian-friendly Thai dish. Enjoy the combination of the tender eggplant, aromatic basil, and savory stir-fry sauce!

Khanom Krok (Coconut Pancakes)

Ingredients:

For the Batter:

- 1 cup rice flour
- 1/2 cup all-purpose flour
- 1 cup coconut milk
- 1 1/2 cups water
- 1/2 teaspoon salt
- 1 tablespoon sugar

For the Filling:

- 1 cup coconut cream
- 1/2 cup palm sugar (or brown sugar), finely chopped
- 1/4 teaspoon salt

Instructions:

In a mixing bowl, combine rice flour, all-purpose flour, coconut milk, water, salt, and sugar. Whisk the ingredients together until you have a smooth batter. Let the batter rest for at least 30 minutes to allow it to slightly thicken.

In a separate saucepan, heat the coconut cream over medium heat. Add the finely chopped palm sugar and salt to the coconut cream. Stir continuously until the sugar dissolves and the mixture thickens slightly. Set aside.

Preheat a Khanom Krok pan or a similar pan with small, round molds. If you don't have a specific Khanom Krok pan, you can use a mini pancake pan or aebleskiver pan.

Grease the molds with a small amount of oil to prevent sticking.

Pour a small amount of the batter into each mold, filling them about halfway.

Once the edges of the pancakes start to set, add a small spoonful of the coconut and palm sugar mixture into the center of each pancake.

Cover the pan and let the Khanom Krok cook for 5-7 minutes or until the edges are crispy and golden brown. You can use a skewer or fork to lift the edges slightly and check the doneness.

Once the edges are crispy, use a spoon to carefully flip each pancake, creating the characteristic half-moon shape.

Cook for an additional 5-7 minutes on the other side until fully cooked and golden brown.

Remove the Khanom Krok from the pan and repeat the process until all the batter is used.

Serve Khanom Krok warm, allowing the coconut and palm sugar filling to be creamy and slightly gooey. Enjoy these delightful coconut pancakes as a sweet treat or dessert!

Chicken and Cashew Nut Stir-Fry

Ingredients:

For the Stir-Fry Sauce:

- 3 tablespoons oyster sauce
- 2 tablespoons soy sauce
- 1 tablespoon fish sauce
- 1 tablespoon sugar
- 1 tablespoon water

For the Stir-Fry:

- 1 lb (about 500g) boneless, skinless chicken breasts or thighs, cut into bite-sized pieces
- Salt and pepper to taste
- 2 tablespoons vegetable oil
- 3 cloves garlic, minced
- 1 red bell pepper, sliced
- 1 yellow bell pepper, sliced
- 1 cup snow peas, ends trimmed
- 1 cup baby corn, halved
- 1 cup broccoli florets, blanched
- 1 cup unsalted cashews
- Green onions, chopped, for garnish (optional)
- Cooked rice, for serving

Instructions:

In a small bowl, whisk together the oyster sauce, soy sauce, fish sauce, sugar, and water to create the stir-fry sauce. Set aside.
Season the chicken pieces with salt and pepper.
Heat the vegetable oil in a wok or a large skillet over medium-high heat.
Add the minced garlic and sauté for about 30 seconds until fragrant.
Add the seasoned chicken to the wok and stir-fry until the chicken is fully cooked and browned on the edges. This usually takes about 5-7 minutes.

Add the sliced bell peppers, snow peas, baby corn, and blanched broccoli to the wok. Continue to stir-fry for an additional 3-4 minutes until the vegetables are tender-crisp.

Pour the prepared stir-fry sauce over the chicken and vegetables. Stir well to coat everything in the sauce.

Add the unsalted cashews to the wok and toss them with the chicken and vegetables.

Cook for an additional 2-3 minutes until the sauce thickens slightly, and the cashews are heated through.

Remove the wok from heat. Garnish the stir-fry with chopped green onions if desired.

Serve the Chicken and Cashew Nut Stir-Fry over cooked rice.

Enjoy this delicious Thai stir-fry with the perfect balance of savory, sweet, and nutty flavors!

Thai Beef Salad

Ingredients:

For the Beef:

- 1 lb (450g) sirloin or flank steak
- Salt and black pepper, to taste
- 1 tablespoon vegetable oil

For the Salad:

- 1 cup cherry tomatoes, halved
- 1 cucumber, thinly sliced
- 1 red onion, thinly sliced
- 1 cup fresh cilantro leaves, chopped
- 1 cup fresh mint leaves, torn
- 1 cup fresh basil leaves, torn

For the Dressing:

- 3 tablespoons fish sauce
- 2 tablespoons lime juice
- 1 tablespoon soy sauce
- 1 tablespoon sugar
- 1-2 Thai bird chilies, finely chopped (adjust to taste)
- 2 cloves garlic, minced

Optional Garnish:

- Roasted peanuts, crushed
- Sesame seeds

Instructions:

Season the steak with salt and black pepper on both sides.

Heat vegetable oil in a grill pan or skillet over medium-high heat. Cook the steak for about 3-4 minutes per side for medium-rare, or adjust the cooking time to your desired doneness. Let the steak rest for a few minutes before slicing it thinly against the grain.

In a large bowl, combine the cherry tomatoes, sliced cucumber, red onion, cilantro, mint, and basil.

Prepare the dressing by whisking together fish sauce, lime juice, soy sauce, sugar, chopped Thai bird chilies, and minced garlic in a small bowl.

Add the sliced beef to the salad and drizzle the dressing over the top. Toss everything gently to combine, ensuring that the beef and vegetables are well coated with the dressing.

Garnish the Thai Beef Salad with crushed roasted peanuts and sesame seeds if desired.

Serve the salad immediately, allowing the flavors to meld together.

This Thai Beef Salad offers a perfect balance of savory, tangy, and herbaceous flavors.

It's a refreshing and satisfying dish that can be enjoyed on its own or with a side of rice.

Gaeng Som (Sour Curry)

Ingredients:

For the Curry Paste:

- 5-8 dried red chilies, soaked in warm water
- 2 shallots, peeled and chopped
- 4 cloves garlic, peeled
- 1 stalk lemongrass, white part only, thinly sliced
- 1 tablespoon galangal, sliced
- 1 tablespoon shrimp paste (kapi)
- 1 teaspoon ground turmeric

For the Sour Curry:

- 1 cup mixed vegetables (such as Thai eggplant, long beans, pumpkin, bamboo shoots), chopped
- 200g shrimp or fish fillets, cleaned and deveined (optional)
- 3-4 cups water or vegetable broth
- 2 tablespoons tamarind paste
- 1 tablespoon fish sauce
- 1 tablespoon palm sugar or brown sugar
- Salt, to taste
- Fresh cilantro leaves, for garnish

Instructions:

Start by making the curry paste. In a blender or mortar and pestle, combine the soaked dried red chilies, shallots, garlic, lemongrass, galangal, shrimp paste, and ground turmeric. Blend or grind into a smooth paste.

In a pot, heat a small amount of oil over medium heat. Add the curry paste and sauté for a few minutes until fragrant.

Add the mixed vegetables to the pot and stir well to coat them with the curry paste.

Pour in water or vegetable broth, enough to cover the vegetables. Bring the mixture to a boil and let it simmer until the vegetables are tender.

Add tamarind paste, fish sauce, and palm sugar to the pot. Adjust the seasoning with salt if needed.

If you're using shrimp or fish, add them to the pot and cook until they are just cooked through.

Allow the curry to simmer for a few more minutes, ensuring that all the flavors meld together.

Taste the curry and adjust the sourness, sweetness, or saltiness according to your preference.

Garnish the Gaeng Som with fresh cilantro leaves.

Serve the Thai Sour Curry hot over steamed rice.

Gaeng Som is known for its vibrant flavors, with the combination of sour, salty, and sweet notes. It's a versatile dish, and you can adjust the ingredients and spice level to suit your taste preferences. Enjoy!

Kanom Jeen Nam Ya (Rice Noodles with Fish Curry)

Ingredients:

For the Rice Noodles (Kanom Jeen):

- 2 cups rice flour
- 3 cups water
- 1/2 teaspoon salt
- Banana leaves or parchment paper, for steaming

For the Fish Curry (Nam Ya):

- 400g fish fillets (snakehead fish is commonly used)
- 1 can (400ml) coconut milk
- 3 tablespoons red curry paste
- 2 tablespoons fish sauce
- 1 tablespoon palm sugar or brown sugar
- 1 teaspoon shrimp paste (kapi)
- 1-2 kaffir lime leaves, torn into pieces
- 1-2 Thai bird chilies, chopped (adjust to taste)
- 1 tablespoon vegetable oil
- 1 cup water

For Serving:

- Bean sprouts
- Fresh cilantro leaves
- Sliced red onion
- Lime wedges

Instructions:

Start by making the rice noodles (Kanom Jeen). In a bowl, mix rice flour, water, and salt until you have a smooth batter.
Prepare a steamer and line the steaming trays with banana leaves or parchment paper.

Pour a thin layer of the batter onto the trays, spreading it evenly. Steam for about 5-7 minutes or until the noodles are cooked through. Repeat the process until all the batter is used.

Once the noodles are cooked, allow them to cool slightly, then cut them into manageable lengths.

For the fish curry (Nam Ya), blend the fish fillets into a smooth paste using a food processor or blender.

Heat vegetable oil in a pot over medium heat. Add the red curry paste and sauté for a few minutes until fragrant.

Add the fish paste to the pot and cook, stirring constantly, until it starts to release its oils and becomes aromatic.

Pour in the coconut milk and water, stirring to combine.

Add fish sauce, palm sugar, shrimp paste, torn kaffir lime leaves, and chopped Thai bird chilies. Bring the curry to a gentle simmer and cook for about 15-20 minutes, allowing the flavors to meld together.

Taste the curry and adjust the seasoning if needed.

To serve, place a portion of rice noodles in each bowl and ladle the fish curry over the top.

Garnish with bean sprouts, fresh cilantro leaves, sliced red onion, and lime wedges.

Enjoy Kanom Jeen Nam Ya, a delightful Thai dish that combines the unique flavors of rice noodles and fragrant fish curry!

Kai Jeow Moo Sab (Pork Omelette)

Ingredients:

- 150g ground pork
- 3 large eggs
- 2 cloves garlic, minced
- 1 tablespoon fish sauce
- 1 tablespoon soy sauce
- 1 teaspoon oyster sauce
- 1/2 teaspoon sugar
- 1/4 teaspoon black pepper
- Vegetable oil for frying
- Fresh cilantro leaves, for garnish (optional)
- Sliced green onions, for garnish (optional)

Instructions:

In a bowl, combine the ground pork, minced garlic, fish sauce, soy sauce, oyster sauce, sugar, and black pepper. Mix well to ensure the pork is evenly coated with the seasonings.
Heat a non-stick skillet or wok over medium heat and add a tablespoon of vegetable oil.
Add the seasoned ground pork to the pan and cook, breaking it up with a spatula, until it is browned and cooked through.
In a separate bowl, beat the eggs.
Push the cooked pork to one side of the pan, add a bit more oil if needed, and pour the beaten eggs into the empty side of the pan.
Allow the eggs to set for a moment, and then gently scramble them. As the eggs begin to set but are still slightly runny, combine them with the cooked pork.
Continue cooking, stirring occasionally, until the eggs are fully cooked and the omelette is well combined.
Taste and adjust the seasoning if needed, adding more fish sauce or soy sauce according to your preference.
Once the omelette is cooked to your liking, transfer it to a serving plate.
Garnish with fresh cilantro leaves and sliced green onions if desired.

Serve the Kai Jeow Moo Sab hot with steamed rice or enjoy it on its own as a tasty and satisfying dish. It's a quick and versatile recipe that can be customized to suit your taste preferences.

Kao Niew Mamuang (Mango Sticky Rice)

Ingredients:

For the Sticky Rice:

- 1 cup glutinous rice
- 1 cup coconut milk
- 1/2 cup sugar
- 1/2 teaspoon salt

For the Coconut Sauce:

- 1 cup coconut milk
- 2 tablespoons sugar
- 1/4 teaspoon salt

For Serving:

- Ripe mango, peeled, pitted, and sliced
- Sesame seeds, toasted (optional)
- Mung beans, steamed (optional)

Instructions:

Rinse the glutinous rice under cold water until the water runs clear. Soak the rice in water for at least 4 hours or overnight.
After soaking, drain the rice.
Steam the glutinous rice in a bamboo or metal steamer lined with cheesecloth or muslin cloth for about 25-30 minutes, or until the rice is tender and fully cooked.
While the rice is steaming, prepare the coconut sauce. In a saucepan, combine coconut milk, sugar, and salt. Heat over medium heat, stirring constantly until the sugar dissolves and the mixture is well combined. Remove from heat and set aside.
Once the sticky rice is cooked, transfer it to a large bowl. While the rice is still hot, pour the coconut milk (for the sticky rice) over it. Mix well until the rice is evenly coated with the coconut milk mixture.

Let the sweet sticky rice sit for 15-20 minutes to allow it to absorb the coconut flavor.

While the rice is resting, prepare the coconut sauce for drizzling. In another saucepan, combine coconut milk, sugar, and salt. Heat over medium heat, stirring constantly until the sugar dissolves. Remove from heat and set aside.

To serve, mold a portion of sweet sticky rice on a plate or in a bowl. Arrange slices of ripe mango on top.

Drizzle the coconut sauce over the mango and sticky rice.

Optionally, garnish with toasted sesame seeds and steamed mung beans.

Serve Kao Niew Mamuang immediately, and enjoy the delightful combination of sweet, creamy, and slightly salty flavors. It's a classic Thai dessert that captures the essence of Thai culinary artistry.

Gang Hung Lay (Northern Thai Pork Curry)

Ingredients:

For the Curry Paste:

- 5 dried red chilies, soaked in warm water
- 5 shallots, peeled and sliced
- 4 cloves garlic, peeled
- 1 tablespoon galangal, sliced
- 1 tablespoon ginger, sliced
- 1 tablespoon shrimp paste (kapi)
- 1 teaspoon ground turmeric

For the Curry:

- 500g pork belly or pork shoulder, cut into bite-sized pieces
- 1 cup pork belly skin, cut into small pieces (optional)
- 2 cups shallots, peeled
- 1 cup garlic, peeled
- 2 tablespoons vegetable oil
- 2 tablespoons tamarind paste
- 2 tablespoons palm sugar or brown sugar
- 2 tablespoons fish sauce
- 1 tablespoon soy sauce
- 1 teaspoon salt
- 4-5 kaffir lime leaves, torn into pieces
- 2 cups water or pork broth
- 1 cup peanuts, roasted and crushed (for garnish)

Instructions:

Start by making the curry paste. In a blender or mortar and pestle, combine soaked dried red chilies, sliced shallots, garlic, galangal, ginger, shrimp paste, and ground turmeric. Blend or grind into a smooth paste.
In a pot or a wok, heat vegetable oil over medium heat. Add the curry paste and sauté for a few minutes until it becomes fragrant.

Add the pork pieces to the pot and stir well to coat them with the curry paste. Cook until the pork is browned on all sides.

Add the pork belly skin pieces (if using), whole shallots, and whole garlic cloves to the pot. Stir and cook for a few more minutes.

Pour in tamarind paste, palm sugar, fish sauce, soy sauce, and salt. Mix well to combine.

Add torn kaffir lime leaves to the pot and pour in water or pork broth. Bring the curry to a gentle simmer.

Cover the pot with a lid and let the curry cook over low heat for at least 1.5 to 2 hours or until the pork is tender. Stir occasionally and add more water if needed.

Taste the curry and adjust the seasoning if needed, adding more tamarind, fish sauce, or sugar to achieve the desired balance of flavors.

Once the pork is tender and the curry has thickened, remove the pot from heat.

Serve Gang Hung Lay hot, garnished with roasted and crushed peanuts. It pairs well with steamed rice or sticky rice.

Enjoy the rich and aromatic flavors of this Northern Thai Pork Curry, a dish that reflects the unique culinary heritage of the region.

Hoy Tod (Thai Mussels Pancake)

Ingredients:

For the Batter:

- 1 cup rice flour
- 1/2 cup all-purpose flour
- 1 cup water
- 2 eggs
- 1 tablespoon fish sauce
- 1 teaspoon soy sauce
- 1/2 teaspoon sugar
- 1/2 teaspoon baking powder

For the Mussels:

- 1 lb (about 500g) fresh mussels, cleaned and debearded
- 3-4 green onions, chopped
- 1 cup bean sprouts, washed and trimmed
- 2-3 sprigs cilantro, chopped

For Frying:

- Vegetable oil

For Serving:

- Thai chili sauce or sweet chili sauce

Instructions:

In a mixing bowl, combine rice flour, all-purpose flour, water, eggs, fish sauce, soy sauce, sugar, and baking powder. Whisk the ingredients together until you have a smooth batter. Set aside.

Clean and debeard the fresh mussels. If the mussels are large, you can chop them into smaller pieces.

Heat a large pan or skillet over medium-high heat. Add a generous amount of vegetable oil for frying.

Once the oil is hot, pour a ladle of the batter into the pan, spreading it evenly to form a pancake.

Place a handful of mussels on top of the batter, distributing them evenly. Sprinkle chopped green onions, bean sprouts, and cilantro over the mussels.

Allow the pancake to cook until the edges become crispy and golden brown. Use a spatula to check the bottom, making sure it's cooked before flipping.

Carefully flip the pancake and cook the other side until it becomes crispy and golden brown.

Once both sides are cooked and the mussels are cooked through, transfer the Hoy Tod to a serving plate.

Repeat the process with the remaining batter and mussels.

Serve the Thai Mussels Pancake hot, with Thai chili sauce or sweet chili sauce on the side.

Enjoy Hoy Tod as a delicious and crispy Thai street food experience at home. It's perfect for sharing and makes a tasty appetizer or snack.

Kaeng Liang (Vegetable Soup)

Ingredients:

- 4 cups mixed vegetables (e.g., pumpkin, zucchini, yardlong beans, Napa cabbage, Thai eggplant), chopped
- 1 cup sliced bamboo shoots (fresh or canned)
- 1 cup Thai basil leaves, torn
- 1 cup bok choy or spinach, chopped
- 1 cup straw mushrooms or oyster mushrooms, halved
- 1 cup water spinach (morning glory) or watercress, cut into 2-inch pieces
- 2-3 Thai bird chilies, sliced (adjust to taste)
- 4 cups vegetable or chicken broth
- 1 tablespoon vegetable oil
- 3 cloves garlic, minced
- 2 tablespoons soy sauce
- 1 tablespoon fish sauce (omit for a vegetarian version)
- 1 teaspoon sugar
- Salt, to taste

Instructions:

In a pot, heat vegetable oil over medium heat. Add minced garlic and sliced Thai bird chilies. Sauté for about 30 seconds until fragrant.

Add the mixed vegetables and bamboo shoots to the pot. Stir and cook for a few minutes until the vegetables start to soften.

Pour in the vegetable or chicken broth, soy sauce, fish sauce (if using), and sugar. Stir well to combine.

Bring the soup to a simmer and let it cook for 10-15 minutes, allowing the vegetables to cook through.

Add sliced mushrooms, Thai basil leaves, bok choy or spinach, and water spinach or watercress to the pot. Stir gently to incorporate.

Taste the soup and adjust the seasoning with salt, soy sauce, or fish sauce if needed.

Simmer for an additional 5-7 minutes until all the vegetables are tender but still vibrant and retain their texture.

Remove the pot from heat. Serve Kaeng Liang hot, either as a soup on its own or over steamed rice.

Feel free to customize the vegetables based on what you have available or your preferences. Kaeng Liang is a versatile and nutritious dish, offering a wonderful medley of flavors and textures.

Pad Phrik Khing Tofu (Stir-Fried Tofu)

Ingredients:

- 1 block firm tofu, pressed and cubed
- 200g long beans, cut into 2-inch pieces
- 2 tablespoons red curry paste (store-bought or homemade)
- 1 tablespoon vegetable oil
- 2 kaffir lime leaves, finely sliced (optional)
- 1 red bell pepper, sliced (optional, for added color)
- 1 tablespoon soy sauce
- 1 teaspoon sugar
- 1/2 cup Thai basil leaves (holy basil) or regular basil
- Red chili slices, for garnish (optional)

Instructions:

Press the tofu to remove excess moisture, then cut it into cubes.
In a wok or large pan, heat vegetable oil over medium heat.
Add the red curry paste to the hot oil and stir-fry for a minute until it becomes fragrant.
Add the cubed tofu to the wok and stir-fry until the tofu starts to brown slightly.
Add the long beans to the wok and continue stir-frying for another 3-5 minutes until the beans are tender but still crisp.
If using, add sliced red bell pepper for added color and flavor. Stir-fry for an additional 2 minutes.
Season the stir-fry with soy sauce and sugar. Mix well to coat the tofu and vegetables.
Add sliced kaffir lime leaves (if using) and Thai basil leaves to the wok. Stir-fry for another minute until the herbs are wilted.
Taste the dish and adjust the seasoning if needed, adding more soy sauce or sugar according to your preference.
Once everything is well-cooked and seasoned, remove the wok from heat.
Garnish the Pad Phrik Khing Tofu with red chili slices if you like it extra spicy.

Serve the stir-fried tofu and long beans over steamed rice, and enjoy the aromatic and spicy flavors of this Thai dish. Pad Phrik Khing Tofu makes for a satisfying and flavorful vegetarian or vegan meal.

Gaeng Om (Northern Thai Curry Soup)

Ingredients:

For the Curry Paste:

- 5-8 dried red chilies, soaked in warm water
- 4-5 cloves garlic
- 2 shallots, peeled
- 1 tablespoon galangal, sliced
- 1 tablespoon lemongrass, sliced (only the bottom part)
- 1 teaspoon shrimp paste (kapi)
- 1 teaspoon salt

For the Soup:

- 500g meat of your choice (chicken, pork, or beef), thinly sliced
- 1 cup mushrooms, sliced
- 1 cup bamboo shoots, sliced
- 1 cup cherry tomatoes, halved
- 1 cup eggplant, sliced
- 1 cup long beans, cut into 2-inch pieces
- 4-5 kaffir lime leaves, torn into pieces
- 1 cup Thai basil leaves, torn
- 1 tablespoon fish sauce
- 1 tablespoon soy sauce
- 1 tablespoon oyster sauce (optional)
- 1 tablespoon vegetable oil
- 1.5 liters water or broth

Instructions:

Start by making the curry paste. In a blender or mortar and pestle, combine soaked dried red chilies, garlic, shallots, galangal, lemongrass, shrimp paste, and salt. Blend or grind into a smooth paste.

Heat vegetable oil in a pot over medium heat. Add the curry paste and sauté for a few minutes until it becomes fragrant.

Add the thinly sliced meat to the pot and stir until the meat is cooked and coated with the curry paste.

Pour water or broth into the pot, stirring to combine with the curry paste.

Once the soup comes to a simmer, add sliced mushrooms, bamboo shoots, cherry tomatoes, eggplant, and long beans. Stir well.

Season the soup with fish sauce, soy sauce, and oyster sauce (if using). Adjust the seasoning according to your taste.

Add torn kaffir lime leaves to the soup and let it simmer for 15-20 minutes, allowing the flavors to meld together and the vegetables to cook through.

Just before serving, add Thai basil leaves to the pot. Stir and cook for an additional 1-2 minutes until the basil wilts.

Remove the pot from heat and serve the Gaeng Om hot.

Enjoy this hearty and aromatic Northern Thai Curry Soup with steamed rice or rice noodles. The combination of herbs and spices in Gaeng Om creates a unique and delightful flavor experience.

Pla Nung Manao (Steamed Fish with Lime)

Ingredients:

- 1 whole fish (such as sea bass or snapper), cleaned and scaled
- 3-4 stalks lemongrass, bruised
- 4-5 kaffir lime leaves, torn into pieces
- 1 thumb-sized piece of ginger, thinly sliced
- 3-4 Thai bird chilies, sliced (adjust to taste)
- 3 cloves garlic, minced
- 2 tablespoons fish sauce
- 2 tablespoons soy sauce
- 2 tablespoons oyster sauce
- 1 tablespoon sugar
- Juice of 3-4 limes
- Fresh cilantro leaves, for garnish
- Spring onions (scallions), chopped, for garnish (optional)

Instructions:

Clean and scale the whole fish, and make a few diagonal cuts on each side.
In a large steaming dish or on a plate that fits into your steamer, lay down a bed of lemongrass stalks for the fish to rest on.
Place the whole fish on top of the lemongrass.
In a bowl, mix together kaffir lime leaves, sliced ginger, Thai bird chilies, minced garlic, fish sauce, soy sauce, oyster sauce, sugar, and lime juice. Stir until the sugar is dissolved.
Pour the lime sauce over the fish, making sure to coat it inside the cavity and on the skin.
Bring water to a boil in your steamer, and then place the dish with the fish in the steamer. Steam the fish for about 15-20 minutes or until it is cooked through. The cooking time will depend on the size and thickness of the fish.
Once the fish is cooked, remove it from the steamer.
Garnish the Pla Nung Manao with fresh cilantro leaves and chopped spring onions.
Serve the steamed fish hot, either on its own or with steamed jasmine rice.

Enjoy the delicate and aromatic flavors of Pla Nung Manao, a delightful Thai dish that highlights the natural taste of the fish with a zesty lime-infused sauce.

Khao Khluk Kapi (Fried Rice with Shrimp Paste)

Ingredients:

For the Fried Rice:

- 3 cups cooked jasmine rice (preferably cold and day-old)
- 3 tablespoons shrimp paste (kapi)
- 2 tablespoons vegetable oil
- 2 cloves garlic, minced
- 2 eggs, beaten
- 200g small shrimp, peeled and deveined
- 1 cup diced firm tofu
- 1 cup shredded raw green papaya
- 1 cup green beans, thinly sliced
- 1 cup shredded raw mango (optional)
- 1 cup chopped Chinese chives (or green onions)
- 1 cup bean sprouts
- Lime wedges, for serving

For the Accompaniments:

- Sliced cucumber
- Sliced shallots
- Sliced red chili
- Chopped cilantro
- Crushed peanuts
- Fish sauce
- Sugar

Instructions:

Start by preparing the accompaniments. Slice the cucumber, shallots, and red chili. Chop cilantro and crush peanuts. Set aside.
In a wok or large skillet, heat vegetable oil over medium heat.
Add minced garlic and shrimp paste (kapi) to the wok. Stir-fry for a minute until fragrant.
Add diced tofu to the wok and stir-fry until it starts to brown.

Push the tofu to one side of the wok, pour the beaten eggs into the empty side, and scramble them until cooked.

Add shrimp to the wok and cook until they turn pink and opaque.

Add shredded green papaya, green beans, and shredded raw mango (if using) to the wok. Stir-fry for a few minutes until the vegetables are slightly tender.

Add cold, day-old jasmine rice to the wok. Break up any clumps and stir-fry to combine with the other ingredients.

Continue to stir-fry until the rice is heated through and well-coated with the shrimp paste and other flavors.

Add chopped Chinese chives and bean sprouts to the wok. Stir-fry for an additional minute.

Taste the fried rice and adjust the seasoning if needed. You can add a bit more shrimp paste, fish sauce, or sugar to balance the flavors.

Once everything is well-mixed and heated through, remove the wok from heat.

Serve Khao Khluk Kapi hot, with lime wedges and the prepared accompaniments on the side.

To enjoy, squeeze lime over the fried rice and mix in your desired accompaniments. Khao Khluk Kapi is a delightful explosion of flavors, combining the umami richness of shrimp paste with the freshness of the accompanying vegetables and herbs.

Thai Custard (Sangkhaya)

Ingredients:

- 1 cup coconut milk
- 4 large eggs
- 1/2 cup palm sugar or brown sugar
- 1/4 teaspoon salt
- Pandan leaves or vanilla extract for flavor (optional)
- Freshly grated coconut for garnish (optional)

Instructions:

In a mixing bowl, whisk together coconut milk, eggs, sugar, and salt until well combined. If using pandan leaves for flavor, tie them into a knot and add them to the mixture. Alternatively, you can add a few drops of vanilla extract.

Strain the mixture through a fine sieve into another bowl to ensure a smooth custard.

Prepare individual custard cups or a heatproof dish by lightly greasing them with oil.

Pour the custard mixture into the cups or dish.

Create a water bath for steaming by placing the custard cups or dish in a larger pan filled with water, ensuring that the water level is about halfway up the sides of the cups or dish.

Steam the custard over medium heat for approximately 30-40 minutes or until the custard is set. You can test the custard by inserting a toothpick into the center; if it comes out clean, the custard is ready.

Once cooked, remove the custard from the steamer and let it cool to room temperature.

Optionally, garnish the custard with freshly grated coconut before serving.

Thai Custard can be served warm or chilled, and it pairs wonderfully with sticky rice or on its own.

Enjoy the rich and velvety texture of Thai Custard, a delightful treat that showcases the sweet and aromatic flavors of coconut and palm sugar.